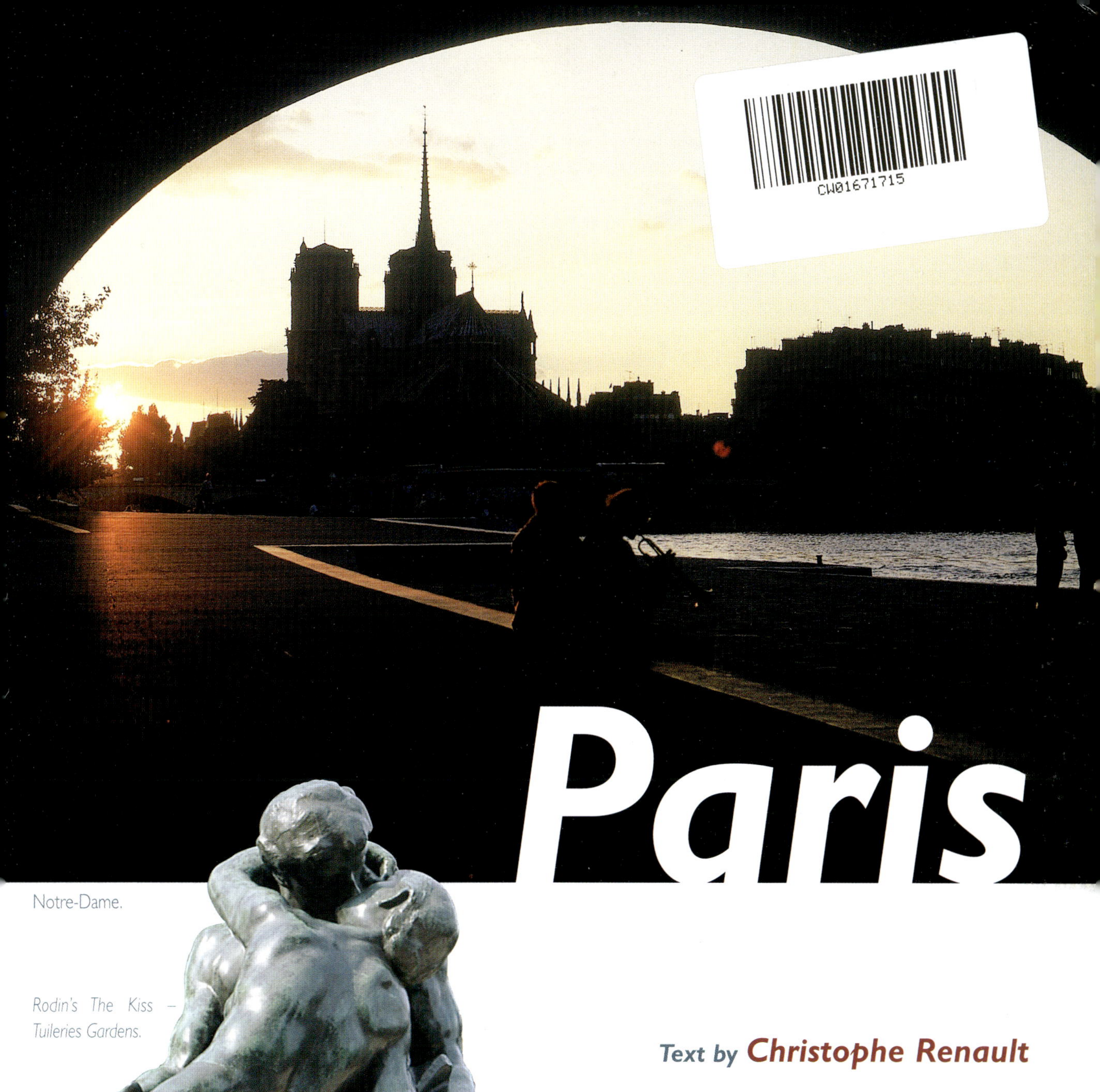

Paris

Notre-Dame.

Rodin's The Kiss – Tuileries Gardens.

Text by Christophe Renault

Translated by Angela Caldwell

Photographs by Jean-Paul Gisserot and Christophe Renault

Éditions Jean-Paul Gisserot
www.editions-gisserot.com

Saint-Denis
La Défense
St-Germain-en-Laye
Malmaison
Versailles
Vincennes
Vaux-le-Vicomte
Fontainebleau
Cité des Sciences et de l'Industrie
Géode
LA VILLETTE
Grande Halle
Rotonde de la Villette
BUTTES CHAUMONT
BELLEVILLE
MÉNILMONTANT
CANAL ST-MARTIN
Gare du Nord
Gare de l'Est
Cimetière de Montmartre
Sacré-Cœur
MONTMARTRE
BATIGNOLLES
Le Moulin Rouge
PIGALLE
Palais des Congrès
ÉTOILE
St.-Augustin
Arc de Triomphe
CHAMPS-ÉLYSÉES
Palais de l'Élysée
La Madeleine
Opéra Garnier
Bourse
Porte St-Martin
Porte St-Denis
Saint-Martin-des-Champs
RÉPUBLIQUE
Musée Guimet
Grand Palais
Petit Palais
Place de la Concorde
Place Vendôme
St-Roch
Comédie française
Palais Royal
Place des Victoires
Hôtel de Soubise
Carnavalet
Cimetière du Père Lachaise
TROCADÉRO
Palais de Tokyo
Pont Alexandre III
Jeu de Paume et Orangerie
Jardin des Tuileries
Le Louvre
LES HALLES
Centre Pompidou
Palais de Chaillot
Musée du Quai Branly
Assemblée Nationale
Musée d'Orsay
St-Germain-l'Auxerrois
Pont Neuf
Place Dauphine
Place du Châtelet et Tour St-Jacques
Hôtel de Ville
LE MARAIS
Place des Vosges
PASSY
Tour Eiffel
CHAMP DE MARS
Hôtel des Invalides
Musée Rodin
Hôtel des Monnaies
Institut
Conciergerie, Ste-Chapelle, Palais de Justice, Tribunal de Commerce
St-Gervais-St-Protais
St-Paul-St-Louis
Hôtel-Dieu
Notre-Dame
École Militaire
St-Germain-des-Prés
Île St-Louis
BASTILLE
NATION
AUTEUIL
BEAUGRENELLE
QUARTIER LATIN
St-Sulpice
La Sorbonne
Musée de Cluny
Palais du Luxembourg
Panthéon
St-Étienne-du-Mont
MOUFFETARD
Muséum National d'Histoire Naturelle
MONTPARNASSE
Val-de-Grâce
Arènes de Lutèce
Pitié-Salpêtrière
BERCY
Observatoire de Paris
GOBELINS
Place Denfert-Rochereau
Catacombes
Bibliothèque Nationale de France
Palais des Sports
LA BUTTE AUX CAILLES
1
2
3
4
5
6
7
8
9
10

Paris in the 13th century, in the days of King Philip Augustus.

The history of Paris
began on Ile de la Cité...

Stone Age man lived on the Ile de la Cité in 5,000 B.C. In the third century B.C, a Celtic people, the Parisii, established a settlement called Lutetia here. It was a strategic spot which was easily defended. After the Battle of Lutetia in 52 B.C, the Romans extended the settlement along the left bank and built a harbour on the right bank. In the 3rd century A.D, Lutetia became the "Town of the Parisii" and, at the end of the 5th century, it took the name "Paris".

During the Dark Ages, the town kept itself very much to itself because of the great Viking and Germanic invasions. In 486 A.D. Clovis came to the fore in Gaul and defeated the last representative of Roman rule.

We recommend Serge Prigent's book Paris, Dates, Facts and Figures from the same publisher.

Illustrations : Top to bottom, left to right : The Institut de France ; Place des Vosges; Notre-Dame de Paris ; The guardroom in the Conciergerie ; The Eiffel Tower ; Les Invalides ; Saint-Denis abbey church ; The Square Courtyard in the Louvre ; One of Hittorff's fountains on Place de la Concorde ; The Medici Fountain in the gardens of the Luxembourg Palace ; The Pantheon ; The Conciergerie.

The accession of Hugh Capet in 987 A.D. made Paris a capital and the town was further organised by Philip Augustus between 1180 and 1223 when he commissioned the building of a wall and a fortress - the Louvre. In those days, Paris covered an area of 272 hectares.

The Parisians gradually began to cluster around the great abbeys located outside the town walls and, when war returned in the 14th century, Charles V had a new wall erected consisting of earth embankments and moats to protect these communities. The town's area increased to 439 hectares.

20 th century : An Art nouveau doorway by Jules Lavirotte.

In the 16th century, Charles V's wall was demolished. Charles IX, however, well aware of the ever-present sense of insecurity, had a new wall built encompassing the town's 567 hectares.

In the 17th century, Louis XIV had the old walls demolished since they no longer served any purpose. In the 18th century, a new type of wall appeared, this time designed to force people entering the town to pay a toll. This wall, which was completed in 1787, was called the "Tax Collectors' Wall". It was three to five metres high (10 to 16 ft.) and it surrounded a town covering an area of 3,370 hectares.

In 1841, Thiers commissioned one last wall to encircle Paris. It was 36 km (22 miles) long and was designed to withstand attack from outside the city which, by then, had a population of 1.7 million and covered an area of 7,088 hectares. Fifteen years later, Haussmann modernised Paris and opened up wide avenues. The extension of Paris was finished and the suburbs, which have developed in the 20th century, form the final ramparts of a city which now covers 8,692.5 hectares.

Middle Ages : Notre-Dame de Paris.

Notre-Dame : the two towers, the rose window in the south transept, the spire above the transept crossing and the chevet flanked by its flying buttresses.

Tour n° 1

An imaginary bird on a Notre-Dame balustrade.

1

Notre-Dame

Cité

Maurice de Sully, Bishop of Paris between 1160 and 1196, was ordered to rebuild the old Notre-Dame Church and turn it into a sumptuous Gothic cathedral worthy of the parish of the Kings of France.

The chancel and transept were completed in 1182. The High Altar was consecrated in the same year by the Bishop of Paris assisted by a papal legate.

Building work on the nave was completed at the end of the 12th century and this enabled the construction of the two towers, which were finished c. 1250. It was also at that time, in the first half of the 13th century, that the single-arch flying buttresses were added to the walls of the nave. The clerestory was enlarged, as demanded by the Flamboyant Gothic style, and a spire was built above the transept crossing.

History has not retained the name of the first architect but the names of the men who designed the façades of the transept are known.

2

1 : The nave and chancel of the cathedral.
2 : The transept crossing.

Right : The south side of the cathedral.

"Notre-Dame as an architectural monument is not one of those which can be called complete, definite, belonging to a class. It is no longer a Romanesque, nor is it yet Gothic. This edifice is not a typical one. [...] Every face, every stone, of this venerable monument, is a page not only of the history of the country, but of the history of science and art."

The Hunchback of Notre Dame - Victor Hugo (1899 translation).

Jean de Chelles was commissioned to build the façades in 1250. He completely built the entrance in the north arm of the transept, called the "Cloister Door", and in 1258 began work on St. Stephen's Door to the south; it was later completed by Pierre de Montreuil. At the end of the 13th century and until the beginning of the 14th, radiating chapels were added to the chancel and flying buttresses to the chevet, giving Notre-Dame the appearance that is so characteristic within the history of French Gothic architecture.

During the French Revolution, Notre-Dame was damaged by Parisian rebels and restoration was not to begin until 1841, under Viollet-le-Duc.

The West Front of Notre-Dame has some fine 13th-century carving. The Last Judgement Portal in the centre represents the Resurrection of the Dead and the Weighing of Souls by St. Michael, the Archangel. Christ appears in majesty above them, between the Virgin Mary and St. John. The Virgin Mary Portal on the left celebrates Her resurrection and coronation. In the coving are foliage, flowers, angels, kings, patriarchs and prophets. The St. Anne Portal on the right includes a tympanum carved at the end of the 12th century depicting the Romanesque theme of the Madonna and Child. Mary is flanked by two angels and, according to some historians, by Charles VII and Maurice de Sully. A double lintel was added in the 13th century. It is decorated with scenes from the life of St. Anne and St. Joachim, the Virgin Mary and the Child Jesus. The Nativity scene is easily recognisable.

Left : The south arm of the transept.
Original Sin - the base of the jamb in the left doorway.

Right : The west front.

The archaeological crypt

The digs carried out between 1965 and 1970 on the square in front of Notre-Dame revealed major remains of the town walls and two rooms with hypocausts dating from the Dark Ages. Numerous vernacular and religious constructions built between the Middle Ages and the 18th century were also discovered. The remains of the Merovingian cathedral were brought to light again, revealing a building with five aisles laid out like the great Roman basilicas of the later days of Antiquity. It was decided to turn the site into an archaeological crypt in order to preserve it for posterity.

1

2

3

1 : St. Anne Doorway: general view of the upper section.
2 : Last Judgement Doorway : coving on the right.
3 : The Virgin Mary Pier on the left doorway of the West Front.
4 : Lintels above the Last Judgement Doorway.

4

Hôtel-Dieu

Tribunal de Commerce and Quai aux fleurs

A hospital (Hôtel-Dieu) is known to have stood on the square in front of Notre-Dame as far back as the 9th century but its location has been changed since then. The hospital as we see it today dates from the redesigned layout of modern-day Paris by Baron Haussmann. Between 1864 and 1874, Jacques Gilbert was responsible for re-erecting an Italianate Classical building based on the hygienist design drawn up in 1854 for the Lariboisière Hospital. Stanislas Diet continued the work until 1877. There was then a delay before completion. The hygienist doctors questioned the position and orientation of the building and the layout of its rooms and wards, which they considered to be too narrow. In 1874, the upper storey was demolished, the ventilation was improved and the first patients were admitted in 1877.

Cité

Quai aux Fleurs

The district to the north-east of the Ile de la Cité remains free of Haussmann's new designs. The houses between the quayside and Notre-Dame Cathedral give a romantic impression of what the island looked like before Haussmann launched his project.

Napoleon III planned to build administrative offices on the Ile de la Cité and place them under the control of Church and State. Gilbert's designs for the hospital were originally neo-Gothic to emphasise the close ties between these two authorities. The Emperor, however, preferred the neo-Tuscan style.

◄ The bridge (Petit-Pont) leading to the hospital.

▼ The Commercial Court (Tribunal de Commerce), Conciergerie and bridge (Pont-au-Change).

The Bonbec Tower (right) is the oldest tower in the Conciergerie, dating from the 13th century. The 14th-century Caesar and Silver Towers are twin towers flanking the north side of the guardroom.

During the Revolution Quenn Marie-Antoinette, Charlotte Corday, Robespierre and Danton were jailed in this building.

Conciergerie

Cité

The palace of the Merovingian kings stood on the site of a Gallo-Roman citadel and was rebuilt on the orders of Philip Augustus (1180-1223). It was also during his reign that strong walls were built around the city of Paris.

Between the end of the 13th and the beginning of the 14th centuries, Philip the Fair (1285-1314) commissioned extensions to the palace, to house the kingdom's financial, administrative and legal offices in the new Gothic buildings. The names of the architects are known - Jean de Cérens (or d'Esserent) followed by Nicolas de Chaumes and Jean de Saint-Germer.

Three large chambers built in the 14th century have survived – the Chamber of the Men at Arms, the Guardroom and the kitchen. The Chamber of the Men at Arms (1301-1312) is of impressive proportions. It is 69.30 metres in length and 27.40 metres wide with a floor-to-ceiling height of 8.55 metres. Three rows of robust pillars separate the chamber into four areas. Four fireplaces provided the heating for the chamber, which was used as a refectory by palace staff. The Guardroom is 22.80 long and 11.80 metres wide with a floor-to-ceiling height of 6.90 metres. Three pillars divide this chamber into two areas, with four spans set on intersecting ribs. The capitals are decorated with carvings of animals and human heads.

At the corner of Rue de Harlay and Quai de l'Horloge is the Clock Tower built during the reign of John the Good (1350-1364). It housed the first public clock in Paris, brought into service circa 1370 during the reign of Charles V (1364-1380).

In the 14th century, the Louvre became the king's main place of residence and the palace then housed the Law Courts. It was placed under the command of the king's governor, the Concierge, who was responsible for the prison attached to the court.

The lead-covered cedarwood steeple rising to a height of 33 metres above the roof dates from the restoration work undertaken by Lassus in the 19th century, as does the painted decoration. The great West Rose Window was totally rebuilt between 1485 and 1498 on the orders of King Charles VIII.

All the stained-glass windows in the upper chapel are separated from each other by a narrow stone framework that marks out the nave. The chapel is 36 metres (117 ft.) long and 17 metres (55 ft.) wide. The height up to the vaulting of this delicate nave is 20.50 metres (67 ft.).

The lower chapel.
The painted elements in Sainte-Chapelle were restored during the XIXth century. Only a few scenes painted on the walls date from the origin.

Sainte-Chapelle

Cité

The Sainte-Chapelle was built by the future St. Louis (1214-1270) to house the Crown of Thorns and relics of the True Cross which he received from Emperor Baudouin II of Constantinople. It would appear that the building was commissioned c. 1241 and consecrated in 1248. The chapel is a veritable reliquary in glass, consisting of two chapels, one above the other, the upper chapel and lower chapel. The upper chapel, reserved for worship by the royal family, leads directly into the rooms in the palace. It is 20.50 m. (67 ft.) high. The lower chapel, used by the palace servants, is 6.60 m. (21 ft.) high.

The Law Courts

and bridge (Pont au Change)

Cité

The Law Courts (Palais de Justice) were rebuilt by Antoine, Desmaisons, Moreau and Couture after being damaged by fire in 1776. The architects decided to recreate the forms of the Renaissance period and 17th century, based on the porticos and colonnades of Greek temples. The central area of the Courts which open onto the May Courtyard includes a monumental flight of steps leading to a portico topped by an entablature decorated with four Allegories. In 1783, the courtyard was closed off by a wrought-iron gate decorated with antique motifs, fleurs de lys and the royal coat-of-arms.

Pont-au-Change

In 1141, moneylenders and goldsmiths were authorised by King Louis VII to set up shop on the original wooden bridge which the monarch crossed on his way to Notre-Dame. Legend has it that the royal procession was accompanied by a flock of thousands of birds released by bird sellers. The present bridge was built in the 19th century as part of Haussmann's new city design.

Place Dauphine

Cité or Pont-Neuf

Henri IV decided to have a triangular square built on the western section of the Ile de la Cité as part of a plan to redesign the area including the bridge (Pont Neuf), the tip of the Ile de la Cité and Rue Dauphine. The king ceded the new land created by backfilling the tip of the island to the President of the Parliament, Achile de Harlay, who lived in the adjacent mansion, now the Law Courts.

The square, which was built in the same period as Place des Vosges, includes thirty-two stone and brick houses with slate roofs.

It was called Place Dauphine in honour of Henri IV's eldest son.

Louis Métezeau was probably the architect responsible for providing the triangular layout of the square in 1874 when it was altered by the architect of the west wall of the Law Courts.

Each house has a galleried ground floor, two square storeys and an attic floor beneath the slate roof. The two pavilions leading into Place Dauphine from the bridge (Pont Neuf) and facing the equestrian statue of King Henri IV are the only two surviving original examples of the square's houses.

▲ The pavilions leading onto Place Dauphine from the bridge (Pont Neuf).

The destruction of 1874

Harlay's Lobby, the west side of the Law Courts, was designed by Joseph-Louis Duc in 1869. It overlooked Place Dauphine but, since one side of the square prevented people getting a clear view of his building, he decided to have that side of the square demolished in 1874.

Pont-Neuf

The Pont Neuf (1578-1607) has undergone countless restorations. It was Henri III who laid the foundation stone. The bridge quickly became a popular place for a motley crowd of merchants, jugglers, charlatans and passers-by. Booksellers set up stalls there in 1619 before moving to the river banks in later years.

▲ Mary of Medici decides to have a statue erected in honour of her husband, Henry IV. She asks her uncle Ferdinand I of Tuscany for advice and he commissions John of Bologna for the job. The scultor dies in 1608. The statue is completed in 1611 and shipped to France in 1613. It is unveiled on the Pont Neuf in 1614 by Louis XIII. The statue was smashed during the French Revolution and replaced by a statue by Lemot in 1818.

Île Saint-Louis

Pont-Marie or Sully-Morland

The layout of the Ile Saint-Louis dates from the 17th century. The first chapel was built in 1622. In 1642, it was decided to replace it. The designs for the construction of St. Louis' Church were commissioned from François Le Vau. The foundation stone of the chancel was laid in 1664 and the building was consecrated in 1679. The foundation stone for the nave was laid in 1702 under the direction of Gabriel Le Duc. The old chapel adjacent to the chancel had been used as a nave until then. Jacques Doucet replaced Gabriel le Duc after his death in 1702. The bell tower, which was completed in 1765 replaced a bell tower above the transept crossing which had been struck by lightning in 1760. The name of the architect of the new tower is not known.

The furnishings inside the church are quite outstanding. Most of the works of art were brought here by Father Bossuet, parish priest from 1864 to 1888.

Pont Marie, the bridge connecting Ile Saint-Louis to the city.

Quai de Béthune gets its name from Maximilien de Béthune, better known as Sully, minister to Henri IV. A number of private mansions deserve particular attention. No. 24 was built for Helena Rubinstein in the 20th century, on the site of a 17th-century building. President Georges Pompidou died there in 1974. Only the 17th-century entrance was retained and integrated into the mansion we see today.

Hôtel Lambert on the Île Saint-Louis ▼.

The mansion at N°. 51 Rue Saint-Louis-en-l'Île is a 17th-century building purchased in 1719 by Jean-François Guyot de Chenizot, General Inspector of Finance from Rouen. Pierre Vigné de Vigny altered the façade overlooking the street in 1726, adding Rococo-style motifs. The dragon brackets, animals' heads and ornamental rococo features are a remarkable example of a style that was rare in France. ▼

The Richelieu Pavilion in the Louvre.

Tour n°2

A centaur ridden by Love. A Roman replica of an original work created in the 2nd century B.C. in Asia Minor – Louvre Museum.

Louvre or Palais-Royal

Two carvings of Fame holding Henri II's royal shield by Jean Goujon, on the tympanum of the central frontispiece in the Lescot Wing (Square Courtyard). ▶

The east wing of Philip Augustus' palace in the Louvre.

The Louvre

Philip Augustus had a tall keep built in 1190, in front of the town walls. It was to protect the right bank of Paris; it was also designed as a symbol of royal authority.

It was Charles V who, in the 14th century, first took up residence in the Louvre. The very famous miniature from the "Très Riches Heures du duc de Berry" shows the refurbishment work carried out by Raymond du Temple, the king's architect, in the 1360's. The fortress then accommodated the royal family and its suite, even though the palace on the Ile de la Cité remained the official residence.

François I had the keep demolished in 1528 and began restoring and refurbishing the mediaeval fortress to give it the palatial appearance we see today. In 1546, François I commissioned architect Pierre Lescot to rebuild the royal residence. The Louvre Palace laid out for Charles V was to be replaced by a building with the same design, i.e. four sides. The carvings on the façades were created by Jean Goujon. This was the first example of Renaissance art in Paris; it was continued by Henri II after the death of François I and gave rise to the square courtyard (Cour carrée).

After the Grand Gallery commissioned by Catherine de Medici from Louis Métezeau and Androuet Du Cerceau to link the Louvre and the Tuileries Palace, it was Louis XIII who continued François I's work by adding a wing to counterbalance the

The Victory of Samothrace. This statue represents the Greek goddess Athena Nike. Athena brought victory in the 4th or 3rd century B.C. ▶

Pont des Arts (1801-1804) is an iron bridge built during the Napoleonic Empire. It was rebuilt, in steel, in 1982-84. ▶▶

1

2

The Square Courtyard : The façade was designed by Pierre Lescot and Jean Goujon (west wing). A new architectural style is apparent in this wing. The pilastered rectangular projections set into the wall, the columns, the rectangular pediments and the curves are regularly spaced across the façade, creating a perfect rhythm. Cartridges with scrolls or indentations inspired by the leatherwork of the Fontainebleau School add to the decoration. Some of the smaller ones are further decorated with the crowned "H" cipher of King Henri II or with an "H" intertwined with the "C" of Catherine de Medici.

3

one built by Pierre Lescot. Louis XIII ordered Jacques Lemercier to continue the inner courtyard which then had only two façades, on the west and south. The foundation stone of the new pavilion, the Clock Pavilion, was laid on 15th July 1624.

The caryatids on the upper storey were carved by Jacques Sarrazin who also oversaw the decoration work.

Le Vau replaced Lemercier upon the latter's death in 1654 and continued the renovation and refurbishment of the palace.

1 : Lemercier Wing, the extension of the Lescot Wing in the Square Courtyard.

2 : The Clock Pavilion overlooking the Square Courtyard.

3 : The west wing (left) in the Square Courtyard dates from the Renaissance period.

Claude Perrault was chosen to build a monumental façade in the Classical style opposite the church of Saint-German l'Auxerrois. Its design was diametrically opposed to the Baroque excesses suggested by Bernini and initially accepted. The Colonnade, on which work began in 1670, marked the beginnings of the Second Classical period in France.

1

2

3

In 1682, the king moved from the Louvre to Versailles, leaving behind him a palace in which some of the buildings had no roofs. Faced with this slow deterioration, the new king, Louis XV, ordered Gabriel and, later, Soufflot, to restore the abandoned palace. At that time the north and south wings in the square courtyard were still roofless.

In the Consular period and during the Empire, Napoleon ordered Pierre-François Fontaine and Charles Mercier to begin work on the north wing of the palace, along Rue de Rivoli, and to complete the upper storeys of the north and south wings in the Square Courtyard. The two architects also designed a copy of the Arch of Septimus Severus which was erected on Place du Carrousel between 1806 and 1808.

From 1815 onwards and during the Restoration of the Monarchy, the Bourbons paid little attention to the Louvre. It was the Republic of 1848 that finally approved the linking of the Tuileries and Louvre palaces but it was Napoleon III who had the honour of adding the finishing touches to the great plans initially commissioned by kings. Visconti, who died very early, and Lefuel were the driving forces behind the completion of this long-standing project. On 23rd May 1871, the Paris Commune set fire to the Tuileries but the Louvre was spared. The Third Republic decided to demolish it, opening the Louvre up to the Champs-Elysées and Arc de Triomphe.

1 : Work began on the colonnade designed by Claude Perrault in the 1670's. This marked the beginnings of the Second Classical Period in France.
2 : General view of the Carrousel Arch.
3 : Victory Driving a Chariot by Pierre Cartellier (central projecting section of the Colonnade).

One century later, François Mitterand decided to make the Louvre the largest museum in the world. The museum then occupied the entire palace and the huge pyramid more than 20 metres (62 ft.) high was built to designs by architect Ieoh Ming Pei in the centre of the Napoleon Courtyard. It was inaugurated in 1989.

The Museum's collections

Egyptian Antiquities

▲ Egyptian sphinxes from the Ptolemaic era.

◄ Pharaoh Ramses II, 1279 - 1213 B.C. 19th dynasty.

Oriental Antiquities

▲ Winged androcephalus bull. Low reliefs from the palace of Sargon II of Assyria. Decoration from the town and the King's palace in Dur-Sharrukin, now Khorsabad near Mossul.

Roman antiquities

Back of the so-called "Trees" sarcophagus. Rome, early 4th century. ►

"A Harvesting Cherub". Mosaic. Carthage, 4th century A.D. ▼

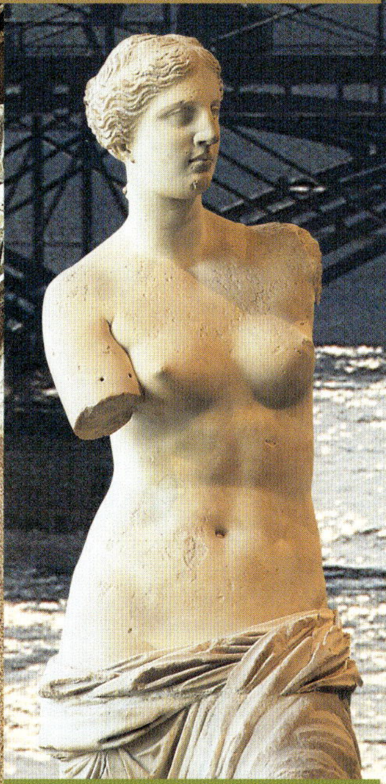

Greek Antiquities

▲ The "Venus de Milo". Milo (Cyclades Islands), circa 100 B.C.

Northern European Art

▲ "The Astronomer" by Johannes Vermeer alias Vermeer of Delft (1632-1675).

Italian Art

▲ "Mona Lisa" by Leonardo de Vinci (1452-1519). The painting was stolen from the Louvre in 1911 in an incredible manner and found in Florence. The event greatly increased the work's popularity.

"The Mystic Marriage of St. Catherine" (close-up) by Antonio Allegri alias Correggio (1489-1534). ▼

Spanish Art

"The Young Beggar" by Bartolome Esteban Murillo (1618-1682).

French Art

◄◄ "The Lock", by Jean-Honoré Fragonard (1732-1806).

◄ "Pierrot", formerly known as "Gilles", by Jean-Antoine Watteau (1684-1721).

"Liberty Guiding the People" by Eugène Delacroix (1798-1863), 1831 Salon. ▼

Italian Sculpture

▲ "The Rebel Slave" (1513-15) by Michelangelo (1475-1564).

French Sculpture

Reception pieces for the Royal Academy of Sculpture. ▼

Tuileries or Concorde

Only a few traces have survived in Paris – in the Tuileries Gardens, the Art School (École des Beaux-Arts), the Trocadéro Gardens, Square Georges-Cain in Rue Payenne, n° 9 Rue Murillo, n° 254 and n° 266 Boulevard Raspail and n° 28 Rue des Saints-Pères.

The Tuileries, named after the local tileworks, used to consist of a central, domed building flanked by side wings ending in small pavilions.

The gardens between the Tuileries Palace and today's Place de la Concorde were commissioned from André Le Nôtre in 1664 by Colbert, then Minister to Louis XIV.

Fame and Mercury riding Pegasus were made by Antoine Coysevow. They, too, decorated the drinking-troughs in the Château de Marly. They now stand at the entrance to the Tuileries Gardens. ▼

The Tuileries

Musée du Jeu de Paume and Musée de l'Orangerie (art galleries)

In 1563, after Henri II's death, Catherine de Medici ordered the construction of a new residence in the west of Paris, outside the walls and not far from the Louvre. The work was commissioned from Philibert Delorme and, later, from Jean Bullant in 1570.

Catherine de Medici decided, very early on in the project, to link the Tuileries and Louvre by means of a gallery almost 470 metres (510 yds.) long. The plan has gone down in history as the "Grand Intention" but it was not completed until the end of the Second Empire, in 1860.

The castle was set on fire in1871, during the Paris Commune. It stood in ruins until 1882 when the Parliament decided to raze it to the ground.

All that remains of the palace are the two pavilions i.e. The Flora Pavilion overlooking the Seine and the Marsan Pavilion on Rue de Rivoli.

The Tuileries Gardens are now one vast open-air museum of sculpture.

The Orangery beside the Seine dates from 1853. It houses the prestigious collection of late 19th and early 20th century paintings put together by Jean Walter and Paul Guillaume. Claude Monet's "Water Lilies" are also on display here. The Musée du Jeu de Paume on Rue de Rivoli was built in 1861 and inspired by the layout of the Orangery. The hall was successively an exhibition hall then an annex of the Louvre Museum, used to display works by the Impressionnists. When the Orsay Museum was opened, having been designed to house the 19th-century collections, the Jeu de Paume was used for temporary exhibitions of contemporary works.

Saint-Germain-l'Auxerrois

and the Town Hall of the 1st arrondissement

This was the parish church of the Kings of France because of its closeness to the Louvre.

The church we see today dates from the 13th century. The nave, transept and side aisles were rebuilt in the 15th century, as was the Burgundian-style doorway, between 1431 and 1439. The chancel, built circa 1250, underwent alteration in the 16th century.

The entrance dates from the first half of the 13th century and is an outstanding example of mediaeval Parisian sculpture. The six statues on its well-preserved jambs represent figures from the Old Testament and saints from the diocese.

Between 1858 and 1860, Jacques-Ignace Hittorff designed an architectural composition in the style of the day, creating a building inspired by the symmetry of the church for use as the Town Hall of the 1st arrondissement, or district. Built in the Gothic style and a highly-skilful example of religious architecture used in a modern way to create a vernacular building devoid of rules and doctrines, this construction was the result of an eclectic approach to the project.

Louvre

It is a sad fact that the bells on Saint-Germain-l'Auxerrois were used as a signal to launch the St. Bartholomew Massacre on the night of 24th to 25th August 1572.

A roodscreen designed by Pierre Lescot and Jean Goujon in the early 16th century was destroyed in 1754.

◄ Saint-Germain-l'Auxerrois (15th century).

Mary the Egyptian (15th century) in the Church of Saint-Germain l'Auxerrois. ▼

The neo-Gothic belfry designed by Théodore Ballu between 1858 and 1862 is wrongfully said to be the church tower.

Place Vendôme (1699-1720)

Concorde

Jules Hardouin-Mansart built, on the site of a mansion belonging to the Duc de Vendôme, an octagonal square flanked by colossal façades displaying the Corinthian order and harmonious Classical proportions. During the Empire, Napoleon followed in the footsteps of Roman emperors by having a commemorative column erected (1806-1810) in the style of the Trajan Column. It took the bronze from 1,200 enemy cannon to clad the 44-metre (143 ft.) column.

The Vendôme Column was erected in 1810 in the centre of the square by architects Jacques Gondouin and Jean-Baptiste Lepère. Its design was based on the Trajan Column in Rome. The low relief carved by Étienne Bergeret represents the 1806 campaign. The column, which was topped by a statue of Napoleon by Antoine-Denis Chaudet, was replaced by a replica made by Auguste Dumont in 1873, after the original column had been demolished by supporters of the Paris Commune.

The housefronts on Place des Victoires and Place Vendôme are examples of the "colossal" order which consists of a tall basement with cross walls pierced with semi-circular windows and, above this, columns or pilasters stretching up past two storeys or more. The same architectural concept can also be seen in Versailles.

Saint-Roch

The first church on this site was completed in 1588 and was a daughter-church of Saint-Germain-L'Auxerrois. It was dedicated to the five wounds of Christ and to St. Roch.

The plans for the new church were commissioned from Jacques Le Mercier in 1653, shortly before his death. Work began in 1670 after the original church had been demolished and continued, with difficulties, until 1690 when the chancel and transept were completed.

In 1705, Jules Hardouin-Mansart began the construction of the Lady Chapel adjoining Le Mercier's chevet. The layout is very unusual, consisting of a central elliptical nave flanked by an ambulatory in which the open areas are linked by a set of arches. The light flooding into the chapel forms a dramatic contrast with the darkness of the chancel. Pierre Bulet completed the chapel after Hardouin-Mansart's death, placing an opening in the rear wall of the chapel.

In 1690, the nave and chancel were roofed with temporary timber vaulting. The roof was completed in 1722 and funded by Law the financier.

In 1738 Robert de Cotte built the West Front in a style influenced by the Baroque. In the mid 18th century, in fact in 1754, Étienne-Louis Boullée extended the church by adding the Calvary Chapel. This brought the overall length of the church to 120 metres.

Pyramides

Saint-Roch.

The Church of St. Roch contains a large number of works of art, for example paintings by Théodore Chassériau ("The Baptism of the Eunuch" and "St. Francis Xavier Baptising an Indian" (1853)); a monument to Father de l'Epée by architect Jean-Baptiste Lassus and sculptor Auguste Préault (1840); a bust of André Le Nôtre by Antoine Coysevox (1707); "The Resurrection of the Son of the Widow of Naïm" by Eustache Le Sueur (circa1650); "Godefroy de Bouillon" by Claude Vignon (circa 1620) etc.

The nave and vaulting were completed thanks to the generosity of John Law, who later converted to Roman Catholicism.

Palais Royal

La Comédie française and the seat of the Council of State

Palais-Royal

Cardinal de Richelieu commissioned architect Jacques Le Mercier in 1630 to build a mansion which he bequeathed, upon his death, to King Louis XIII. When the king died, Anne of Austria occupied the mansion with her court and enjoyed a luxurious lifestyle. In 1692, the mansion became the property of Monsieur, Louis XIV's brother.

Monsieur had Hardouin-Mansart extend the gallery on Rue de Richelieu as far as the main garden. This was the happiest period in the history of the Palais-Royal with entertainments, drama productions and music.

The façades overlooking the Clock Courtyard were altered by Moreau-Despoux in 1763. From 1781 to 1784, the gardens were flanked by two wings designed by Victor Louis. Bookshops, restaurants and cafés opened there, creating hustle and bustle. Betwenn 1817 and 1835, Fontaine the architect designed the wings on each side of the main courtyard. In 1985-1986, sculptor Daniel Buren laid out a series of black and white columns in the main courtyard.

Camille Desmoulins harangued the crowd on 12th July 1789, standing on a table in the Café de Foy in the Palais-Royal. Today, the Palais-Royal is the seat of the Council of State.

1 : The wing of the Palais-Royal designed by Victor Louis.
2 : The gardens of the Palais-Royal.
3 : The Palais-Royal is now the seat of the Council of State.
4 : Rue de Rivoli - It was decided to lay out Rue de Rivoli in 1801, in accordance with a project put forward by architects Charles Percier and Pierre Fontaine. The section between Place de la Concorde and Place du Palais-Royal was opened in 1802. The nearby Place des Pyramides includes a statue of Joan of Arc by sculptor Emmanuel Frémiet. It dates from 1874.

1

2

3

La Comédie française

The Théâtre Français is adjacent to the left wing of the Palais-Royal. A passageway leads into the main courtyard. The theatre was built by Victor Louis from 1786 to 1790.

It was in 1680 that Louis XIV decided to amalgamate the two theatre companies working in the Hôtel de Bourgogne and Rue de Guénégaud. The two companies became one, with premises in Rue des Fossés-Saint-Germain, now Rue de l'Ancienne-Comédie. In 1689, the company took the name "Comédie Française". In 1770, the actors worked in the Tuileries then in the Théâtre de l'Odéon and, finally, in the premises still occupied by the Comédie Française today.

4

Palais de la Bourse

Bourse

In 1808, Napoleon decided to commission a "palatial imperial stock exchange" and Alexandre-Théodore Brongniart designed a temple surrounded on all sides by Corinthian columns. The work was completed by Éloi Labarre and Hippolyte Lebas between 1813 and 1826. A metal roof was installed in 1815. The great central hall is decorated by grisaille paintings by Abel de Pujol and Charles Meynier.

In 1851-1852, allegorical statues were added to each side of the two flights of steps. On the west side stand Commerce and Justice by Augustin Dumont and Francisque-Joseph Duret; on the east side, Agriculture and Industry by Charles-Émile Seurre and James Pradier.

The building rapidly became too small and Jean-Baptiste Cavel was commissioned to extend it between 1902 and 1907. Two wings now flank the central building surrounded by a forest of columns.

The building at n°4 Place de la Bourse was built in 1930 by Gaston Bernier in the Art deco style.

Place des Victoires (1685-1686)

Concorde

The Duc de la Feuillade commissioned Jules Hardouin-Mansart in 1685 to design a round harmoniously-proportioned circus in which the radius of the circle was equal to double the height of the statue. The pedestrian statue by Desjardins was replaced in the 19th century by an equestrian statue by Bosio.

In 1681 the Duc de Feuillade commissioned Desjardins the sculptor to create a statue of Louis XIV for the palace at Versailles, in celebration of the Peace of Nijmegen. He decided to have a replica of the statue erected on the new Place des Victoires.

A sculpture of Colbert by Antoine Coysevox in the chancel of the Church of Saint-Eustache.

Tour n°3

Sanctuary in the Church of Saint-Eustache.

Covered market («Les Halles»)

Châtelet - Les Halles

Louis VI created the Champeaux Market in 1137. Philip Augustus had two long buildings erected in 1183 ; they were called the covered market ("Les Halles") and were designed for the storage and sale of products and produce. A third market was built in 1265. Two fish markets were then built, again during the reign of St. Louis. The market enjoyed extraordinary expansion and rapidly became a major trading centre.

The district was entirely redeveloped between 1854 and 1874, during the Second Empire, by Victor Baltard. However, by the end of the 19th century, the market had become too small and, after numerous expansion or relocation projects, it was decided to seek another site. The market in Rungis opened in 1962. All the traders moved out in 1969 and the inevitable destruction began in 1972.

Paris City Council redeveloped the district by launching another major project and the Forum des Halles opened its doors in 1979.

It was in St. Eustace's Church that the funerals were held of Molière, La Fontaine, Mirabeau and Mozart's mother.

St. Eustace's Church, for which François I laid the foundation stone on 29th August 1532, has the same Gothic layout as Notre-Dame. However, Renaissance decoration was largely and widely introduced. The church is 106 metres (345 ft.) long, 44 metres (143 ft.) wide and 33 metres (107 ft.) high. The building was completed and consecrated on 26th April 1637.

The church still has frescoes by Mignard, paid for by the generous Colbert who was one of its famous parishioners. His tomb can be seen in one of the chapels in the church. It was designed by three artists who worked on Versailles - Charles Lebrun for the drawing, Antoine Coysevox and Jean-Baptiste Tuby for the sculptures. Equally worth seeing are the paintings by two major artists, The Disciples on the Road to Emmaus by Rubens and The Martyrdom of St. Eustace by Simon Vouet.

◄ The Fontaine des Innocents originally stood at the corner of Rue Saint-Denis and Rue Berger. It had three sides decorated, in 1547-1550, by Jean Goujon. In the 18th century, it was moved. Augustin Pajou was commissioned to give it a fourth side. It was then dismantled again. It has stood on its present site since 1865.

◄ The West pediment of the Commodities Exchange.

The Commodities exchange stands on the site of one of Catherine de Medici's palaces. ▼

▼ St. Eustace's Church.

Worth seeing

The monumental staircase tower 27 metres tall serves the various storeys in the mansion. The vaulting above the staircase is decorated with splendid Gothic sculptures representing various plants and symbolising the major members of the Burgundy family e.g. oak for Philip the Bold, hawthorn for his wife, Margaret of Artois, and hops for their son, John the Fearless.

Tour Jean-Sans-Peur

Étienne-Marcel

Robert d'Artois and, later, his daughter Mahaut bought several plots of land in Paris. In the 13th century, he had a mansion built known as the Hôtel d'Artois. After the marriage of Marguerite de Male, Countess of Artois and Philip the Bold, Duke of Burgundy, in 1369 it became the Parisian residence of the Dukes of Burgundy.

After the death of Philip the Bold, John the Fearless had his cousin, the Duke of Orléans, murdered on 23rd November 1407. He had been regent during the reign of King Charles VI the Mad. He then seized power, even succeeding in obtaining absolution for his crime from the king.

To mark this new power, he commissioned a building from Robert de Helbuterne in 1409 on his Parisian estate, "...a large mansion... topped with great Gothic pediments in stone...". It bore his own coat-of-arms and that of his wife. Central to the building was the John the Fearless Tower (tour Jean-Sans-Peur).

Inside, there are several storeys reached by two staircases. On the ground floor is a guardroom (its real function is unknown!); on the first floor a room giving access to the town wall commissioned by Philip Augustus. On the second storey there is a room with ogival vaulting 10 metres tall but little is known about its origins. The third and fourth floors were probably reserved for the duke ad his equerry. These two rooms have latrines. One of the rooms has been restored, with furniture and stained-glass windows.

The spiral staircase leads up to a stone "arbour" decorated with oak, hawthorn and hops foliage, a unique sculptural masterpiece in the Flamboyant Gothic style.

View from the John the Fearless Tower in the 19th century, before restoration.

The John the Fearless Tower has been open to the public since 1999. It houses an exhibition that gives an insight into the history, society and everyday life of Parisians in the early 15th century.

Centre Georges-Pompidou

President Georges Pompidou decided to build a modern art gallery on the Beaubourg Plateau. It was to be attractive to the widest possible cross-section of the general public and to include a library. This was to be more than a place for the people; it was to be a cultural centre specialising in training, education and personal expression.

Italians Renzo Piano and Gianfranco Franchini joined forces with British architect Richard Rogers to present a project in which the structure consisted of five suspended floors, one above the other. Their design was selected in 1971.

The national museum of modern art contains a collection of prestigious works and a tour of the third and fourth floors gives a very wide overview of the main names and trends in contemporary art. Works by Bonnard, Matisse, Derain, Léger, Picasso, Delaunay, Mondrian, Giacometti, Ernst, Dali or, closer to the present day, Soulages, Beuys etc. are hung in a manner designed to make art popular with the general public and accessible to all.

Nearby, on Place Igor-Stravinsky, is the mechanical fountain by Niki de Saint-Phalle and Jean Tinguely, which was inaugurated in 1983. The strange mobiles, representing a red heart, a fire-bird, a nightingale, a snake, a hat and vividly-coloured musical clefs, were designed to pay homage to Stravinsky, composer of The Firebird.

Rambuteau

Nearby, on Place Igor-Stravinsky, is the mechanical fountain designed by Niki de Saint-Phalle and Jean Tinguely, which was inaugurated in 1983. Some fifteen moving sculptures rotate, swing and pour water into a basin measuring 33 metres by 17 metres (107 ft. by 55 ft.).

Châtelet - Les Halles

Tour Saint-Jacques. ▲

Place du Châtelet

Tour Saint-Jacques and Samaritaine

The square came into being in 1130 when Louis the Fat built a small fortress to defend the entrance to the Grand Pont, the bridge now known as the Pont au Change. After the building of the town's outer wall by Philip Augustus, the small fort (or "châtelet") became the seat of jurisdiction for the provost of Paris. It was also the residence of the Provost of Merchants. The fort was later used as a prison, said to have contained numerous torture chambers. The sinister fort was demolished between 1802 and 1810.

The Church of St. James of the Shambles (Saint-Jacques de la Boucherie) was built between 1509 and 1523 to designs by Jean de Felin, in the Flamboyant Gothic style. The church was destroyed in 1797 by its owner, who had purchased it from the State after it had become national property. Only the tower survived and today it stands 52 metres (169 ft.) high, displaying a Flamboyant style consisting of four storeys decorated with tracery and festoons.

The Fontaine du Palmier was commissioned by Napoleon I from Jean-Marie Bralle (1785-1862) in commemoration of victories during the Napoleonic Wars. An initial column-fountain with decorations and a gilded figure of Victory was erected in 1807 on the square created by the demolition of the fortress. In 1860-1862, it was moved to mark the new centre of the square. It was at this time that the four sphinxes were added.

Baron Haussmann commissioned architect Gabriel Davioud to design two theatres, to be built opposite each other on the newly-developed square. The buildings with their neo-Renaissance façades were erected between 1860 and 1862.

View from the Grand-Châtelet which once housed torture chambers, a prison and a mortuary. The sinister castle was demolished in the early 19th century. ▶

1 : The "Palm Tree Fountain" commemorating some of Napoleon's victories. It was commissioned by Emperor Napoleon I in 1807 as a decoration for the new square that was laid out after the demolition of the Grand Châtelet. The sphinxes were added during the Second Empire (1860-1862).

2 : La Samaritaine department store on the banks of the Seine. The frontage (1926-28) was designed by Henri Sauvage. In front of it is the Pont Neuf leading across the river to the Île de la Cité.

3 : Place du Châtelet.

1

2

3

The City-Hall (Hôtel de Ville)

Hôtel-de-Ville

François I commissioned a building in 1532 from Domenico da Cortona, alias Le Boccador and Pierre Chambiges. In 1837, the City Hall (Hôtel de Ville) was altered by architects Godde and Lesueur who added a wing and a pavilion at each end.

Twice in its history, City Hall has provided a refuge for Republicans. They proclaimed the Republic here in 1848, after the fall of Louis-Philippe, and again in 1870 after the fall of Napoleon III in Sedan. On 18th March 1871, Paris capitulated. City Hall was overrun by rioters proclaiming the Commune and the fall of the government. The Paris Commune came into being on 28th March but the ensuing repression was ruthless and its supporters retreated in May, after setting fire to City Hall and the Tuileries Palace.

City Hall was rebuilt between 1873 and 1882 in the same style by Théodore Ballu and Edouard Deperthes.

1

2

1 : Statue of Etienne Marcel.
2 : Etienne Marcel, Provost of Merchants, established the Paris Town Council on Place des Grèves (the original name of Place de l'Hôtel de Ville) on 7th July 1357, in the so-called "House of Pillars".
3 : Pont Notre-Dame.

3

The solitary elm at Saint-Gervais-Saint-Protais.
The presence of a solitary elm tree in a public place in the Middle Ages indicated that justice could be meted out here. An elm was planted in front of the church as a reminder of this custom. **To the left of the church**, at n° 4 and n° 12 Rue François Miron, note the group of buildings designed by Jacques Vinage in 1733. At n° 14 Rue François Miron and n° 17 Rue des Barres, another famous architect, Jacques V Gabriel, father of Jacques-Ange Gabriel, built a number of houses in 1735 for Camuset the barrister. *The elm motif can be seen on the wrought-ironwork on the balconies.*

▲ Anonymous, Our Lady of Pity (19th century), Church of Saint-Gervais-Saint-Protais.

Saint-Gervais-Saint-Protais

Hôtel-de-Ville

Two brothers, St. Gervais and St. Protais, were martyred in Milan during Nero's reign. This parish, which bears their names, probably dates from the 11th century. By the early 14th century, the local people were mainly mariners, regraters, weavers, dyers and tanners. Work on the church we see today lasted from 1494 to 1620. The church was built in the Flamboyant Gothic style with a very tall nave, massive pillars with no capitals to support the huge arches, and vaulting decorated with numerous ribs. Work began on the construction of the West Front in 1616 and lasted until 1620. This was a first in Paris, a forerunner of a style unknown until then in France – Classicism. Salomon de Brosse designed an elevation including three orders, one on top of the other i.e. Doric, Ionic and Corinthian. This marked a return to monumental design in the use of the architectural orders. The work was carried out by Claude Métezeau and Claude Monnard. In 1634, the Church of St. Paul and St. Louis used the idea of the three superimposed orders and the style was imitated for many years thereafter.

Saint-Paul-Saint-Louis

Saint-Paul

This church, originally called St. Louis', was built for the Jesuit professed house; it is now a high school, the Lycée Charlemagne. Originally the building accommodated young men who had taken their religious vows. Building work on the church began in 1627 to designs by Brother Martellange. In 1629, Father François Derand took over and continued to monitor the project until its completion in 1641.

Richelieu celebrated the first Mass in Saint-Paul-Saint-Louis on 9th May 1641.

An inscription placed on the West Front in 1634 recalls the role played by King Louis XIII and Cardinal Richelieu in the building of the church. It reads "Ludovicus XIII Rex basilicam Armandus card. de Richelieu frontemp" (King Louis XIII had the church built and Cardinal de Richelieu the West Front).

Salomon de Brosse (circa 1571-1626) gave a foretaste of French Classicism in the West Front of the Church of St. Gervais in Paris (1616). It marked a return to monumental design in the use of the architectural orders, in this case reaching e over three storeys. Saint-Paul-Saint-Louis, designed by the Jesuit fathers Étienne Martellange and François Derand, continued the work of Salomon de Brosse in 1634 by complying with the concept of three superimposed orders, a style that was copied for many years.

Mansions in the Marais district

The Marais was the aristocratic district during Louis XIII's reign. The aristocracy and rich merchants lived in private mansions given functional and aesthetic coherence from 1630 onwards. The mansions were separated from the streets by a gate and most of them have the same layout. In the centre is the main courtyard; in the wings to right and left are the galleries used for functions and receptions, the service areas and the stables. At the end are the main apartments overlooking both the courtyard and a garden closed off by an orangery. Jean Androuet Du Cerceau used the layout in this particular mansion, built between 1624 and 1630.

Hôtel de Sully, a mansion at n° 62 Rue Saint-Antoine.

The superb recent restoration of the Hôtel de Sully, the head offices of France's Historic Monuments Department.

The Orangery at the end of the garden (right, the doorway leading onto Place des Vosges).

The mansion was named after its owner, Maximilien de Béthune, Duke de Sully, who purchased it in 1634.

Hôtel Le Peletier de Saint-Fargeau (29 Rue de Sévigné). It was built for Michel Le Peletier de Saint-Fargeau in 1688 to designs by Pierre Bullet, architect to the king and the city. The mansion is now an annex of the Carnavalet museum. ▶

Hôtel de Lamoignon (24 Rue Pavée). Diane of France purchased this mansion in 1584 and had it altered by Louis Métezeau. After a break in the work, she had the main section of the mansion completed in 1611-12. The façade with its hunting attributes reflected Diane of France's passionate love of hunting. ▼

▲ **Hôtel d'Aumont** (7 Rue de Jouy). Financier Michel-Antoine Scarron had his own mansion built to plans by François Mansart. Construction began in 1631 and was completed in the 1650's. Catherine, Scarron's daughter, moved into the mansion in 1651 with her husband, Antoine d'Aumont, who bought it in 1655. He asked Charles Le Brun to redesign the interior and, in 1665, had the main stone staircase built by Libéral Bruand. The staircase no longer exists.

▲ The courtyard of the ***Hôtel de Beauvais*** (68 Rue François Miron). The original mansion was built on the site of an early 13th-century residence. A wonderful hall with ogival vaulting remains from this period. In 1654, the property was sold to Pierre de Beauvais and his wife who extended the estate and, in 1656, had a new mansion built to plans by Antoine Le Pautre, architect to the king. The mansion was inaugurated 4 years later.

▲ The façade of the Hôtel d'Albret (31 bis Rue des Francs Bourgeois). The mansion was sold to Charles du Tillet in 1740 and he commissioned architect J.-B. Vautrin to redesign the façade overlooking the street (1741-1744).

Hôtel de Sens (1 Rue du Figuier). This mansion was the Parisian residence of the Archbishops of Sens. From 1475 to 1507, Archbishop Tristan de Salazar had the mansion altered, giving it the layout it has today. In 1605, Margaret of Valois, better known as "Queen Margot", moved into the mansion, staying there until 1606. With the Hôtel de Cluny, the Hôtel de Sens is the largest example of a mediaeval residence in Paris. ▼

The façade overlooking the street.

The gardens.

Saint-Paul or Chemin-Vert

The King's Pavilion has a medallion of Henri IV on the pediment above the first floor. The brackets under the balustraded balcony are very ornate. A frieze of triglyphs, garlands and Henri IV's cipher decorates the pavilion as a whole.

Place des Vosges

In 1605, Henri IV decided to lay out a square flanked on all four sides by arcaded buildings with an identical design. Experts believe that it was Louis Métezeau who designed this Place Royale and had it built between 1607 and 1612. The equestrian statue of Louis XIII was erected in 1639. It was melted down during the French Revolution and a copy was set in its place in 1825.

The square, initially known as Place Royale, was renamed Place des Fédérés then Place de l'Individisibilité. Since 1800, it has been called Place des Vosges, after the first département in France to pay its taxes.

The entire square is characteristic of the architecture of the early 17th century. Red brick and white stone alternate on the austere façades with tall, black slate roofs called, in French, "à la Mansart" after the name of the architect who made their use so popular.

Reconstruction of Fouquet's, the jeweller's shop on Rue Royale.
Musée Carnavalet - Alphonse Mucha - 1900.

Tour n°4

Pierre-François Palloy organised the demolition of the Bastille and, throughout 1790, sent each département (or "county") a carved model of the prison made from its stones.

Musée Carnavalet

Paris historical museum

Saint-Paul

In 1546, Jacques de Ligneris is appointed ambassador to the Council of Trento by King François Ist. In 1547, he commissions architect Nicolas Dupuis to build him a mansion. Pierre Lescot probably supplied the overall design of the builduing. As for Jean Gougeon, he most certainly sculpted the figures of the four seasons on the façade at the back of the courtyard. Françoise de la Baume-Montrevel, the widow of François de Kernevenoc'h, also nicknamed Lord Carnavalet, buys the mansion in 1570. She has a carnival mask sculpted on the portal as well as coats of arms in memory of her husband, who was Henry II's first squire.

Claude Boislève buys the mansion in 1654 and asks François Mansart to supervise the enlargement of the place. Claude Boislève's fall follows that of Fouquet, Louis XIV's Finance Superintendant who is accused of forfeiting Treasury funds. He is jailed and his mansion seized in 1662.

In 1866, the city of Paris buys the mansion, restores it and has it enlarged for the purpose of housing the municipal collections. Three monuments, relics of the old Paris, were transposed to the three sides of Carnavalet gardens: to the South, the arch of Nazareth, built between 1552 and 1556 by Guillaume Le Breton; to the West, the façade of the Office of Drape Merchants erected by Jacques Bruand in 1660 on rue des déchargeurs; to the North, the forefront of the Desmarets mansion, originally erected on rue Saint-Augustin around 1710. In 1989, the municipal museum is extended into the Le Pelletier de Saint Fargeau mansion next door.

Nowadays, in its 140 rooms, the museum presents a collection of paintings, sculptures, furniture and archeological relics related to the History of Paris, including the neolithic wooden boats discovered on a building site in Bercy in 1991.

The main courtyard of Carnavalet mansion and the statue of Louis XIV by Antoine Coysevox.

The façade overlooking the garden was redesigned by Parmentier during restoration work in 1868-70.Also at that time, neo-Renaissance galleries were built, integrating remains of the buildings demolished in the old Paris city centre e.g. to the south a 16th-century pavilion that once straddled Rue de Nazareth on the Ile de la Cité, to the west the façade of the Office of Merchant Drapers built in 1660 in Rue des Déchargeurs and to the north, the central section of the Hôtel des Marets or Hôtel de Choiseul built in Rue Saint-Augustin circa 1710.

Musée Carnavalet

◄ The joust of mariners in front of Notre-Dame bridge, by ***Nicolas Raguenet***.

Attributed to ***Callet Antoine-François*** (Paris, 1741 - Paris, 1823): Nicolas Ledoux (1736-1806), architect, with his daughter Adélaïde. Nicolas Ledoux designed the toll gates erected in the late 18th century around Paris. ▼

◄ ***Claude Lefebvre*** : Marie de Rabutin-Chantal, Marquise de Sévigné (1626-1696). In 1677, the mansion was rented to the Marquise de Sévigné and the famous writer lived in it until her death in 1696. One of the museum's galleries is devoted to her.

▲ ***Hubert Robert*** : The Bastille in the Early Days of its Demolition, July 1789.

Claude Nicolas Ledoux (after) : Wood panelling in the drawing room, Hôtel d'Uzès, 1767. ▶

The Hôtel de Soubise
Musée de l'Histoire de France

Rambuteau

The Soubise mansion (Hôtel de Soubise) was attributed to the National Archives by Napoleon in 1808. The National Archives store the most prestigious documents in the history of France and a "Museum of the History of France" (musée de l'histoire de France) was opened in 1867 to give the general public a chance to see these treasures.

Olivier de Clisson, Constable of France during the reign of Charles V, had a mansion built between courtyard and garden in the years 1371-1375. The Gothic entrance, which has survived, consists of two corbelled towers with a pepperpot roof. The two medallions, carved with the Clission coat-of-arms, date from the restoration work of 1847.

The Hôtel de Clisson, later known as the Hôtel de Guise, was purchased by François de Soubise in 1700. Major work was undertaken by architect Pierre-Alexis Delamair, radically transforming the old mansion. In 1705, the architect launched the construction of the central section of the entrance consisting of two half-moons, back to back, one facing Rue des Francs-Bourgeois and the other facing the courtyard lined, in 1707, by peristyles of columns. The frontage was totally redesigned and given columns backing onto the wall and a huge pediment carved with allegorical figures.

For the interior, Delamair was replaced in 1732 by Germain Boffrand. The two main apartments are among the most beautiful examples of the Rococo style in Europe. An oval pavilion was built in 1735-39. A drawing room occupies each of its two storeys. Ludwig II of Bavaria had the Princess de Soubise' oval drawing room copied in the 19th century and included it as the dining room in his castle at Herrenchiemsee.

Sculptor Jacques Verberckt, who created the wood panelling in Versailles during the reign of Louis XV, also worked on the panelling in the Soubise residence.
The best contemporary painters of mythological scenes and history were commissioned to decorate the panelling. They included François Boucher, Carle Van Loo, Charles Trémolières, Jean Restout and Charles Natoire.

Lake Daumesnil in the Bois de Vincennes.

Tour n°5

The Genius of the Bastille at the top of the July Column.

Bastille

Bastille Between 1370 and 1372, Charles V had a fortress built to defend the town and Hôtel Saint-Pol, once of his residences. Later, Louis XI turned the bastion into a prison. Voltaire and the Marquis de Sade were among those imprisoned here. As a symbol of oppression in pre-Revolutionary France, the Bastille was stormed on 14th July 1789 and immediately demolished by Pierre-François Palloy who had models of the fortress made with stone recovered from the site. Markings in the form of cobblestones now indicate the emplacement of the old prison.

When Louis-Philippe mounted the throne, he expressed a wish to celebrate the Three Glorious Days (27th, 28th and 29th July 1830) which had led to the downfall of his pre-

▲ The 170-tonne column stands on foundations built over the vaulting of the St. Martin Canal which flows into the Arsenal harbour.

decessor, Charles X. He therefore commissioned Jean-Antoine Alavoine and, after 1834, Joseph-Louis Duc to supply a bronze column more than 50 metres (162 ft.) high topped by a statue of the Genius of Liberty by sculptor Dumont. The remains of more than five hundred victims of the 1830 and 1848 revolutions were buried in a vault beneath the column.

The Opéra Bastille was designed by Carlos Ott in 1984 and inaugurated on 14th July 1989 as one of the special events marking the bi-centenary of the French Revolution. The auditorium can seat 2,700 people.

Nation

Nation

The two pavilions on Place de la Nation and the two look-out posts with Doric columns (1785-1787) were once part of the Farmers General Wall (cf. page 64).

They underwent alteration during Louis-Philippe's reign. The statue of Philip Augustus by Antoine Etex and the statue of St. Louis by Augustin Dumont were placed at the top in 1845.

Bercy

Bercy

In the 19th century, boatmen would offload their barrels on the quaysides of Bercy so that they could be stored outside the town walls. This enabled the boatmen to avoid paying toll duties until the goods were sold on. The practice led to the construction of numerous warehouses. Two rows of wine cellars still exist in ***Cour Saint-Émilion***. This is now a bustling area centred on the ***Paris-Bercy multipurpose sports*** centre (1980-84), the park laid out in 1987, the ***Ministry of Finance*** completed in 1990 and the business district. The ***National Library of France*** (Bibliothèque nationale de France) had stood in Rue de Richelieu since the French Revolution but, in 1989, an international tender was launched, an initiative of President François Mitterrand himself. It was the project submitted by architect Dominique Perrault that was finally selected.

The bois de Vincennes

Porte Dorée

▲ Lake Daumesnil in the Bois de Vincennes.

The Bois de Vincennes was the natural, outdoor Law Court of St. Louis who, according to legend, sat under an oak tree when passing judgement. The woodland covers 1,000 hectares and includes an interesting flower garden and fascinating zoo. This was a fashionable spot during the reigns of Louis XIV and Louis XV. Until the Revolution, it was described as a superb "Grand Park". In the early 19th century, Napoleon turned Vincennes Castle into a military fort, leading to unfortunate alterations and destructions. In 1857, Napoleon III and Haussmann envisaged the creation of a park as attractive as the Bois de Boulogne. The project was commissioned from Jean-Charles Alphand who designed an English-style park, contained the lakes and opened up paths to link the main avenues.

The Sacré-Cœur on the hill at Montmartre.

Tour n°6

The Wallace fountains were named after an Englishman, Richard Wallace, who paid for their installation.

Porte Saint-Denis and Porte Saint-Martin

Strasbourg -Saint-Denis

1 : St. Denis Gate.
2 : Trophies on the St. Denis Gate.

1

2

The St. Denis Gate (Porte Saint-Denis) was designed by architect François Blondel in 1672. Commissioned by Paris city council, the decorations and inscriptions on the gate celebrate Louis XIV's victories across the Rhine. The low reliefs above the central archway show the crossing of the Rhine on the south side and the capture of Maastricht on the north side. Sculptors François Girardon and Michel Anguier succeeded each other during the work. On the pillars are various trophies with weaponry.

The St. Martin Gate (Porte Saint-Martin) was commissioned from architect Pierre Bullet in 1674 by the Provost of Merchants. It bears a Latin dedication which reads "To Louis the Great, who twice captured Besançon and Franche-Comté and defeated the German, Spanish and Dutch armies". The four low reliefs flanking the central archway represent the capture of Limburg and the defeat of the German armies on the north side while, on the south side, they depict the capture of Besançon and the breaking of the Triple Alliance. The sculptures were the work of Desjardins, Le Hongre, Marsy and Legros.

Saint-Martin-des-Champs

Conservatoire national des Arts et Métiers

Arts-et-Métiers

The 1850 entrance erected during the extensions added in the 19th century.

The priory of Saint-Martin-des-Champs was founded circa 1060. All that remains of the priory now are the church and refectory. The chancel includes a double ambulatory with radiating chapels; it was built in the 12th century.

The east end of Saint-Martin-des-Champs.

Père Lachaise Cemetery

The layout of the cemetery is more like that of a park than a graveyard. More than 12,000 trees filled with birds welcome Parisians out for their Sunday stroll or tourists with time to spare. However, cemetery it is and it is a popular sightseeing venue because it is the last resting place of famous people from history. The graves of authors Molière and La Fontaine were transferred here in the early 19th century. Beaumarchais, Chopin, Delacroix, Mérimée, Balzac and Edith Piaf are also buried here, as are so many more celebrities.

The Père Lachaise cemetery gets its name from a Jesuit father, François d'Aix de La Chaise, Louis XIV's confessor, who lived on this estate, the property of his order. Paris city council purchased the estate in 1804 to turn it into a model cemetery. It was Alexandre-Théodore Brongniart who designed it. Étienne-Hippolyte Godde built the main entrance circa 1825.

Père Lachaise

Gare du Nord and Gare de l'Est

The railway stations were rebuilt or built during in the mid 19th century as a result of the booming increase in railway traffic.

Gare-du-Nord or Gare-de-l'Est

Gare de l'Est
The station was built between 1847 and 1850 by François-Alexandre Duquesney. It was the terminus for the Paris-Strasbourg line and bore the very poetic name of "Strasbourg embarkation point". It was renamed Gare de l'Est in 1854 when the line to Mulhouse was brought into service. It was extended between 1924 and 1931 by engineer Bertaut.

Gare de l'Est ▲
The first Orient Express left for Constantinople from here on 4th October 1883. Another historic memory dates from the First World War. It was from here that soldiers travelled to the Front after mass mobilisation.

Gare du Nord. The first station was built in 1846. It quickly became inadequate because of the constant changes in rail traffic. Jacques-Ignace Hittorff was commissioned to replace the old building by a much larger, more modern construction. It was built between 1861 and 1864, using the modern materials of the day, glass and iron. The materials were given even greater impact 40 years later when the Grand Palais was built. The stone frontage with Corinthian pilasters topped by statues representing Europe's cities conceals the metallic structure from the interior and the platforms.

Canal Saint-Martin

Colonel Fabien

The St. Martin Canal was built between 1822 and 1825 although it was planned much earlier, in 1802, to link the River Seine to the Ourcq Canal. In the south, its terminus is the Arsenal harbour; in the north, it ends at the Villette Basin.

The St. Martin Canal is 4.5 kms long, with nine locks and metal footbridges designed with Venetian-type curves. The "Customs Footbridge" (passerelle de la Douane) near Rue Léon-Jouhaux is an outstanding example of the ethereal design. It dates from 1860.

The Hôtel du Nord, 102 Quai de Jemmapes, was immortalised in 1938 by Marcel Carné in the film of the same name starring the wonderful French actress, Arletty, in which she spoke the immortal line "Atmosphere ? Atmosphere ? Do I look like I do Atmosphere ?". Yet with a few exceptions, the scenes were filmed in the studios in Billancourt.

Nearby is Rue de la Grange-aux-Belles. It used to lead to the gibbet in Montfaucon, erected at the request of Enguerrand de Marigny who was hung there, as was poet François Villon.

Buttes Chaumont

Buttes-Chaumont

The Buttes-Chaumont area was laid out by engineer Adolphe Alphand between 1864 and 1867, assisted by gardener Barillet-Deschamps, architect Davioud and engineer Belgrand. The park was inaugurated by Napoleon III for the World Fair in 1867. It was designed in accordance with Haussmann's principles and is one of the finest parks in Paris. In the middle of its lake is a rocky islet topped by the "Temple of Cybele", inspired by the temple in the Tivoli Gardens. It stands more than 30 metres above the water. The promontory is linked to the banks by a hanging footbridge 65 metres long and by a brick bridge known as the "Suicides' Bridge".

La Villette

Porte-de-la-Villette or Porte de Pantin

La Villette lies between Porte de la Villette and Porte de Pantin, on land occupied by slaughterhouses after 1867.

The building that houses the Cité des Sciences et de l'Industrie is vast hall 270 metres (293 yds.) in length, 110 metres (119 yds.) wide and 49 metres (159 ft.) high.

The Géode, designed by Fainsilber, was built by Georges Chamayou. It is an enormous reflective sphere made of polished stainless steel; it was inaugurated in 1985. Inside is a cinema in which images are projected onto a 1,000 sq. metre semi-spherical screen, taking the audience on an impressive journey right into the heart of the picture.

The Grande Halle is a fine example of 19th-century metal-framed architecture, combining iron and cast iron. Built in 1867 by Jules de Merindol, the great hall used to contain the ox market. It is now a large multi-purpose hall that can cater for an audience of more than 15,000.

The Cité de la Musique, designed by Christian de Portzamparc, was opened in 1995 and brought into use in 1997. It includes the national academy of music (Conservatoire national de musique), a concert hall, a Museum of Music and a music school.

The Rotunda at La Villette (1786-1787) consists of a huge cylinder with peristyle. The centre of the cylinder is open to the sky. Stalingrad Métro station. Claude-Nicolas Ledoux was commissioned to build a wall round Paris with a view to levying tolls on merchandise in accordance with instructions from the tax inspectors « Fermiers généraux ». Each of the gates in the wall controlled one entrance to the town. Now, all that remains of the system are a few of the pavilions used by employees. The others were demolished during the French Revolution or fell victim to vandalism during the 19th century.

La Villette has become a pleasant area since it was redeveloped and Parisians tend to come here at weekends, with their families or friends, to enjoy a stroll, catch a suntan or take part in sports activities. ▼

Montmartre and Pigalle

Abbesse and Funiculaire

The hill of Montmartre is, with the hill at Belleville, the highest point in the capital city. The origins of this district are the subject of controversy among historians. Some believe it was Mons Martyrium, designed to commemorate the martyrs Dennis, Rustique and Eleuthère; others claim that the name is a deformation of Mons Mercurii and that a temple dedicated to Mercury, the Roman god of trade and travellers, was located here.

Encouraged by the Jesuits, two laymen, Alexandre Legentil and Hubert Rohault de Fleury, vowed to build a basilica for the worship of the Sacred Heart of Jesus. Pope Pius IX approved the project and the National Assembly very quickly authorised the work declaring, in 1873, that this was a building useful to the public at large. The hill at Montmartre was chosen and the competition launched in 1874 was won by Paul Abadie. The first, symbolic stone was laid on 16th June 1875 and the project was funded by public subscription.

The Sacré-Cœur on the hill at Montmartre.

The Sacré-Coeur was built in a Romanesque-Byzantine style. It has a vast white cupola over squinches, designed by Rauline, rising high above Montmartre. The dome reaches a height of 83 metres (270 ft.) and from the lantern tower above it there is one of the finest views of Paris. Lucien Magne built a campanile 80 metres (260 ft.) high and hung in it a huge bell weighing 19 tonnes, the "Savoyarde", brought from Annecy where it was cast on a cart pulled by 28 horses. It was a present from the dioceses of Savoy.

1 and 2 : Saint-Pierre-de-Montmartre is one of the oldest churches in Paris. It was the chapel of the Benedictine nuns who occupied Montmartre's first abbey. It was consecrated on Easter Monday in 1147 by Pope Eugene III.
3 : The Lapin Agile, Rue des Saules.
4 : The steps in Montmartre.
5 : Sacré-Cœur.

Right : The Sacré-Cœur on the hill at Montmartre.

1

4

2

5

3

ANVERS
HOTEL

The cabaret known as "Le Lapin Agile" dates from 1860. Initially called "Le Rendez-vous des Voleurs" then "Le Rendez-vous des Assassins", it changed its name again in 1880 when artist André Gill painted a comical rabbit wearing a cap on the façade. The animal was depicted scrambling out of a saucepan, with a bottle in its paw. In a play on words, Gill's rabbit (the "lapin à Gill") became the agile rabbit (the "lapin agile"). The cabaret became very popular as a centre of Parisian nightlife. Among its customers were the artists Utrillo, Picasso, Modigliani and Vlaminck and writers Max Jacob and Apollinaire.

In the 18th century, the hill boasted more than thirty windmills. The last surviving member of the Debray family had the idea of turning his mill into a dance hall and serving his customers warm pancakes ("galettes") between fashionable dances. The Moulin de la Galette attracted artists and writers who came here to seek solace in a glass of Montmartre's own wine.

The Sacré-Cœur and the Church of St. Peter of Montmartre.

At the mill known as the "Moulin de la Galette", patrons could eat freshly-made pancakes ("galettes") between dances.

The Moulin Rouge was opened in the same year as the Eiffel Tower - 1889. At that time, it was no more than a dance hall but, at the end of the 19th century, it quickly became famous for fashionable entertainment.

Bagatelle, the white "folly" of the Count of Artois.

The bois de Boulogne and Bagatelle

In 1775, Louis XVI's brother the Count of Artois made a wager with Marie-Antoinette that he could have a new country house built in two months by his architect, François-Joseph Bélanger, on his estate in the depths of the Bois de Boulogne. There was already a house here, called "Bagatelle", an allusion to a place famous for debauchery in the 18th century. The grounds were laid out by Thomas Blaikie in an Anglo-Chinese style. Extended and completely changed in the second half of the 19th century, the estate was purchased by Paris City Council in 1905.

The Bois de Boulogne was once a section of the Rouvray Forest which, in the Middle Ages, lay to the north-west of Paris. The woodland gets its name from the church commissioned by Philip the Fair in 1301 in memory of a pilgrimage to Boulogne-sur-Mer. The French Revolution and the installations built by the Allies after defeating Napoleon devastated the wild life in the woodland, which underwent renovation during the mid 19th century by Alphand, Davioud and Barillet-Deschamps. Now, the Bois de Boulogne includes countless footpaths, more than 15 kms of cycle track, 28 kms of bridlepath and two lakes. It is a haven of peace and tranquillity, linked to the chaos of Paris by the beautiful Avenue Foch.

A magnolia.

Crocus in bloom.

Tulips.

Corsican pines in the Parc de Bagatelle.

The main staircase in the Opera House designed by Garnier.

Tour n°7

Arc de Triomphe – Peace (1815) – on the Neuilly side, by Antoine Etex (1808-1888).

The arc de triomphe
and la Défense

Charles-de-Gaulle - Étoile and la Défense

Work began on the Arc de Triomphe in 1806, under the supervision of Chalgrin; it stopped in 1814, at the beginning of the period known as the Hundred Days.

Relaunched by the Bourbon dynasty in 1823, the construction of the Arc de Triomphe was to continue until 29th July 1836, during the reign of Louis-Philippe, thirty years after the foundation stone had been laid. It was then dedicated to the French army between 1789 and 1815.

Chalgrin sought inspiration in the Titus Arch in Rome but designed the Arc de Triomphe in Paris to be more grandiose in size. It is 50 metres tall and 45 metres wide and stands on the Chaillot Hill. Its four enormous pillars are decorated with carvings celebrating the French Revolution and Napoleonic Empire.

On the north pillar facing the Champs-Elysées, François Rude (1784-1855) carved the Departure of the Volunteers in 1792, better-known as The Marseillaise. On the south pillar, Jean-Pierre Corot (1787-1843) created The Triumph of 1810. On the opposite side, Antoine Etex (1808-1888) depicted Resistance (north pillar) and Peace (south pillar). Above these huge high reliefs are six low reliefs representing respectively, Marceau's Funeral, The Battle of Aboukir, The Bridge at Arcole, The Capture of Alexandria, Austerlitz and Jemmapes.

On the entablature at the top of the arch, sculptors depicted The Departure and Return of the French Army and, on the attic, shields engraved with the names of the main victories won during the French Revolution and the Napoleonic Empire.

Since 11th November 1923, the Flame of the Unknown Soldier has flickered here, in memory of all the brave, anonymous heroes of the First World War.

La Défense business district.

The Departure of the Volunteers in 1792 on the north pillar of the Arc de Triomphe. The high-relief, also known as La Marseillaise, was carved by François Rude.

The district known as La Défense gets its name from a monument commemorating the defence of Paris in 1871. The gigantic development project that was to produce this district was launched in 1955 and, in 1958, entrusted to EPAD (Etablissement pour l'aménagement de la Défense). Work began on the first building in 1957 when three architects (Camelot, de Mailly and Zehrfuss) were commissioned to design the C.N.I.T. (Centre National des Industries et Techniques). This contemporary building formed the focus of subsequent development in a district linked to the capital city by a major rail and road network. Although the tall skyscrapers no longer impress anybody, the Arche de la Défense (1983-1989) designed by Danish architect Otto von Spreckelsen is of massive proportions. It is an open cube with sides 100 metres (325 ft.) in length. The open centre is 90 metres (293 ft.) high and 70 metres (228 ft.) wide. The arch has 4,000 windows and is clad with 35,000 marble slabs. Its 300,000 tonnes are supported on 12 piles sunk into the ground to a depth of 30 metres (98 ft.) A main road 7 km (4 1/2 miles) long links the Grande Arche to place de la Concorde.
A major trading and business district covers La Défense. The parvis and the succession of squares, all of them for pedestrians only, constitute a veritable open-air museum of modern art with Icarus by César (1965), the Fontaine des Corolles by Leygue (1973) etc.

The Champs-Élysées

Champs-Élysées-Clemenceau

Colbert ordered André Le Nôtre to redesign the Tuileries Gardens in the 1670's. The man who was to become famous as the landscape designer of Versailles extended the central avenue in the Tuileries Gardens as far as today's Rond-Point des Champs-Elysées. To do so, he cleared a pathway through the undergrowth and marshes that then lay beyond the park in which the palace stood.

In 1724, the "Grand-Cours" was extended to what is now referred to as "l'Etoile" (Place Charles-de-Gaulle) ; it was continued in 1774 to Porte Maillot. No houses stood along it until the 18th century when Gabriel completed the two sumptuous mansions flanking Place de la Concorde, then known as Place Royale. It was, though, in the mid 19th century that the Avenue des Champs-Elysées became filled with hustle and bustle. The bourgeoisie frequented café-concert halls and restaurants and flocked to dance halls such as the Château des Fleurs which were very fashionable in the 1850's. The Avenue des Champs-Elysées is divided into two by the "round-about" designed by Le Nôtre. At the southern end are avenues and gardens filled with people when exhibitions in the Petit and Grand Palais draw in the crowds. At the northern end, towards the Arc de Triomphe, are luxury boutiques, popular stores, cinemas, cafés and fast-food outlets designed to satisfy the requirements of tourists and Parisians alike.

Grand Palais.

The Grand and the Petit Palais

Champs-Élysées-Clemenceau

The Grand Palais was designed for the 1900 World Fair. Charles Girault, who was commissioned to carry through the project, was assisted by Henri Deglane, Albert Louvet and Albert Thomas. The building work took three years to complete (1897-1900).

The Petit Palais (1897-1900), which stands opposite the Grand Palais, was built at the same time as its larger counterpart to designs by Charles Girault, sole architect for this project.

Its main façade is 122 metres (132 yds.) long. In the centre of the palace is a semi-circular, open-air garden 58 metres (63 yds.) in diameter flanked by four walls.

The sculpture on the tympanum above the porch was commissioned from Jean-Antoine Injalbert who created an allegory of Paris, flanked by Muses.

Each of the entrances to the Grand Palaid is decorated with pylons, statues and huge quadriga. The two quadriga at the end of the building indicate the side entrances. They were carved by sculptor Georges Récipon.

Petit Palais.

Alexandre IIIrd bridge

Champs-Élysées-Clemenceau or Invalides

The Pont Alexandre III (1896-1900) was built at an angle so that it was aligned with the Esplanade des Invalides. At each end are two pillars 23 metres (75 ft.) high bearing statues of Fame and Pegasus. Allegorical statues at the base of the pillars represent Renaissance France and the France of Louis XIV (left bank), and the France of Charlemagne and contemporary France (right bank).

Place de la Concorde

Concorde

In 1755, the king's senior architect decided upon the conventional solution of a column and designed the Place Louis XV, now Place de la Concorde. Two palaces (1766-1775) were designed by Gabriel, separated by Rue Royale. Each of the façades has columns and the Corinthian order predominates. The pediments flanked by trophies were carved by Guillaume II Coustou and René-Michel Slodtz. The palace to the right was used as a royal furniture store from 1774 to the French Revolution and now houses the naval high command.

An equestrian statue of Louis XV, initially designed by Bouchardon but completed by Pigalle, stood in the centre of the square. It was replaced by a statue of Liberty during the French Revolution and, very shortly afterwards, by the guillotine which executed 1,119 people including Louis XVI, Marie-Antoinette, Danton and Robespierre. It was not until the Directoire, in 1795, that Place Louis XV took the name Place de la Concorde, as a sign of national reconciliation.

1 : A rostral column on Place de la Concorde.
2 : The eight "lookout posts" that now bear figures representing the largest cities in France were private homes. They had a basement and a garden on the square.

1

2

3

3 : fountain designed by Jacques Hittorff.
4 : The Marly Horses were made by Guillaume Coustou for the drinking-troughs in Marly. They were moved in 1795 and have, since then, decorated the entrance to the Champs-Elysées.
5 : The square and the obelisk.

5

4

Place de la Concorde

The final appearance of the square was decided upon in 1835 during the restoration of the monarchy. The Obelisk from the Temple of Luxor, a gift from Mehemet-Ali, Viceroy of Egypt, in 1831, was placed in the centre of the square between Hittorff's two fountains representing maritime navigation and river navigation. The eight statues symbolising the largest towns in the kingdom and set around the square, like the rostral columns symbolising the town, also date from Louis-Philippe's reign.

La Madeleine

During Louis XV's reign, it was decided to build a domed church dedicated to St. Mary Magdalen to close off the perspective from Place de la Concorde along Rue Royale. The work began in 1764 but was interrupted by the French Revolution and a plethora of alterations slowed the construction work still further. From 1807 onwards, Pierre-Alexandre Vignon (1763-1828) turned the church into a Greco-Roman temple. Napoleon wanted to make it a temple to the glory of the French army. It was completed in 1842, during the reign of Louis-Philippe, and returned to the Church.

The imperial temple is surrounded by 52 fluted Corinthian columns 20 metres (62 ft.) high. The portico is topped by a pediment representing the Last Judgement carved by Philippe-Henri Lemaire. A flight of 28 steps leads to the bronze doors in the main entrance decorated with scenes from the Old Testament. Inside is a single aisle 108 metres (117 yds.) long lit by three domes.

Madeleine

Gabriel Fauré and La Madeleine

In 1874, Fauré deputised for Saint-Saëns as organist in the church dedicated to Mary Magdalen. In April 1877, Théodore Dubois replaced Saint-Saëns as organist and Fauré was appointed Choirmaster. On 21st January 1893, the first version of his Requiem was performed here. The final version was completed in 1900. On 26th October, for the funeral of Charles Gounod, he directed the choir while Saint-Saëns played the great organ.

The pediment on the Madeleine church was designed by sculptor Lemaire.
It represents Mary Magdalen begging Christ on the Day of the Last Judgement. The huge bronze doors depict the Ten Commandments.

Opéra Garnier

Opéra

It was during the period when Haussmann was undertaking his major redevelopment of the city that Charles Garnier (1825-1898) designed this eclectic masterpiece, dressing the Paris Opera House (1862-1875) in the most excessive of Baroque decoration.

Marble of various hues was used for the external decoration, the whites, blues, greens, reds and pinks contrasting sharply with the golden bronze of the ornamental busts and statues.

As part of the decoration, Carpeaux created his sculpture, La Danse, which was placed on the main façade. It was replaced in 1964 by a copy by Paul Belmondo; the original is on view in the Musée d'Orsay. Rossini, Auber, Beethoven, Mozart, Spontini, Meyerbeer and Halévy can also be seen, in effigy, on this temple to the lyric arts.

The auditorium can seat 2,200 people on five levels and the stage, 52 metres (169 ft.) wide and 37 metres (120 ft.) deep for a height of 66 metres (215 ft.) can carry 450 actors.

"The Dance" by Carpeaux.

The interior of Opéra Garnier. The ceiling paintings were commissionned by Malraux and designed by Chagall. ▶

The façade of the Opera House. ▼

The Military Academy (Ecole militaire) designed by Jacques-Ange Gabriel between 1751 and 1773.

Tour n°8

The entrance to the Orsay Station is decorated with sculptures created for the World Fair in 1878. They are allegorical figures representing the Continents. This photograph shows Emmanuel Frémiet's Elephant.

Eiffel Tower
and Champ-de-Mars

Champs-de-Mars-Tour-Eiffel

The Eiffel Tower was designed, like other metallic structures, to show visitors to the 1889 World Fair the advances made in iron architecture.

The Tower, designed by Gustave Eiffel was built between 28th January 1887 and 31st March 1889. It consists of more than 15,000 pieces of iron connected by 2,500,000 rivets. In all, it measures 300 metres (975 ft.) in height and today it is a symbol of Paris.

It was its vital role in the history of communications that saved it from demolition and gave it additional height. In 1936, the first television aerial was installed, to be replaced in 1957 by a more powerful network. This increased the height of the Tower to 320.75 metres (almost 1,059 ft.).

▲ The **Champ-de-Mars** was laid out in 1765 to designs by Jacques-Ange Gabriel. It was used for manoeuvres and parades by the military academy, for hot-air balloon experiments, for revolutionary festivities, for military ceremonials during the Napoleonic Empire, for horse races between 1833 and 1860 and, finally, for World Fairs.

Iéna

The Tokyo Palace (Palais de Tokyo) was built for the International Exhibition of Arts and Technology in 1937. The Paris City Council's Modern Art Gallery (musée d'Art moderne) built up a collection of modern art and opened its doors to the public in 1961.

The Palais Galliéra is a pastiche of an Italian Renaissance palazzo built between 1878 and 1894. It has housed the Fashion and Costume Museum (musée de la Mode and du Costume) since 1977.

The Guimet Museum (Musée Guimet) was commissioned by the State in 1888 to house the collections of Asian art built up by industrialist Émile Guimet.

Pierre Traverse, L'Homme. (Man).

Il dépend de celui qui passe
Que je sois tombe ou trésor
Que je parle ou me taise
Ceci ne tient qu'à toi
Ami n'entre pas sans désir.

Translation of the lines by Paul Valéry on one of the large pavilions in the Palais de Chaillot.

The west wing of the Palais de Chaillot, which houses the Musée de l'Homme (ethnology) and the Musée de la Marine (naval museum).

Palais de Chaillot

Trocadéro

Pasteboard, a reproduction of the Trocadero fort in Andalusia by french troops in 1823, was built in 1826, for a military parade. The mane of the place was then changed over from Chaillot.The Palais de Chaillot was built for the 1937 International Exhibition to designs by Jacques Carlu (1890-1976), Louis-Hippolyte Boileau and Léon Azéma (1888-1966).

The Palais de Chaillot retained the layout of the former Palais de Davioud for economic reasons. Opposite the impressive parvis are two huge curved wings, each ending in a monumental pavilion bearing inscriptions by Paul Valéry.

Jacques Ange Gabriel (1698-1782) officially restored the Classical style of the previous reign. This reaction against Rococo architecture harked back to the Louis XIV style.

Jacques-Anges Gabriel was also responsible for the design of Place de la Concorde.

École Militaire

Champs-de-Mars-Tour-Eiffel

The military academy (école militaire) was designed by Jacques-Ange Gabriel between 1751 and 1773. It includes a central pavilion projecting beyond the line of a long Classical façade overlooking the Champ-de-Mars. The two-storey pavilion is topped by a quadrangular dome and has a portico in the style of Ancient Greek or Roman buildings. This marked the beginnings of Neo-Classicism, a style that was to develop until the 19th century. It was Madame de Pompadour and Intendant Pâris-Duverney who persuaded Louis XV to set up a military academy for the kingdom's impoverished young men wishing to enter the king's service. Bonaparte was a student in the academy in 1784 and 1785.

Hôtel des Invalides and Saint-Louis-des-Invalides

Varenne or Latour-Maubourg

North side of the main courtyard.

The Hôtel des Invalides was set up by royal decree on 24th May 1670. The non-military buildings were commissioned from architect Libéral Bruant between 1671 and 1676. The building was to be used as a military hospital and hospice for war-wounded soldiers. The work was completed in 1678.

Saint-Louis-des Invalides (1676-1690) was designed by architect Jules Hardouin-Mansart who added a domed church to one side of the "Soldiers' Church". It is a parallelogram with two superimposed orders (Doric and Corinthian) on the West Front. Above it is a triangular pediment. On top of the parallelogram is a dome with a very tall drum and a slender lantern turret. Statues of Charlemagne by Nicolas Coustou and St. Louis by Coysevox decorate the first storey. The second storey is decorated with trophies and four allegorical statues.

Inside, the Corinthian order has pride of place. The layout is in the form of a Greek cross, with each arm leading into a round, domed chapel. However, it is the painting in the dome which is the most surprising feature. The pendentives in the cupola depict the Evangelists, painted by Charles de Lafosse; higher up, in the cupola itself, are paintings of the Apostles by Jouvenet and Coypel.

Aerial view of the mansion and the Church of Saint-Louis-des-Invalides.

The Classical West Front of Saint-Louis-des-Invalides designed by Jules Hardouin-Mansart.

1

2

3

4

The façade of Les Invalides is 195 metres in length. The central door, flanked by four Ionic pilasters, is decorated with a huge low-relief representing Louis XIV on horseback, dressed as an ancient Greek or Roman and flanked by allegories of Prudence and Justice. The statues of Minerva and Mars were added in 1734 by Guillaume Coustou.

Behind the façade is the royal courtyard, an immense space measuring 102 metres by 63 metres. The flights of steps with their majestic balustrades and the seemingly endless corridors make this the ideal setting for military parades. The courtyard is flanked on all sides by two-storey buildings with a portico of rounded openings breaking up the line like the cloister of an abbey. The base of the roof is decorated with dormer windows set within trophies and each corner has an enormous horse rearing up on its hind legs.

In a crypt 15 metres in diameter and 6 metres deep immediately beneath the dome is the Bonaparte mausoleum. The red Karelian porphyry tomb on a base made of green Vosges granite was built to designs by Louis-Joachim Visconti and inaugurated in 1861. Twelve allegorical statues pay homage to the Emperor; they symbolise Napoleon's victories.

1 : The main organ in Saint-Louis-des-Invalides.
2 : Guns in front of the church.
3 : Saint-Louis-des-Invalides.
4 : Napoleon's mausoleum.

Musée Rodin - Hôtel Biron

Varenne

Financier Abraham Peyrenc de Moras commissioned "the most superb house in Paris" from Jean Aubert between 1728 and 1730. This breathtaking example of Rococo architecture as it was developed in France is nothing less than a mansion set in a three-hectare park. The south pediment, the masks above the windows and the wood panelling inside the mansion are particularly beautiful. The painted decoration was commissioned from François Lemoyne, Louis XV's premier painter. In 1753, the mansion was bought by Maréchal de Biron who had won fame at the Battle of Fontenoy.

The State purchased the estate in 1911. Rodin, who liked it because he had frequented it with a number of artists, offered to bequeath all his works to the State on condition that a museum be opened in his honour in the Biron Residence. This was done in 1919. Nowadays, the museum organises three temporary exhibitions every year.

Hôtel Biron.

The National Assembly

Assemblée-nationale

Statues of statesmen Sully, L'Hospital, Colbert and D'Aguesseau on the façade. In 1839, Cortot replaced the pediment to the glory of Napoleon by sculptures representing France with Freedom and Order at her side and accompanied by the spirits of Commerce, Agriculture, Peace, War and Eloquence.

The Palais Bourbon was built for the Duchesse de Bourbon, daughter of Louis XIV and Madame de Montespan. Building work began in 1722 under Giardini; after his death, it was continued by Pierre Cailleteau alias Lassurance who died in 1724. The work was taken over by Jean Aubert and Jacques V Gabriel who completed the palace in 1730. It was sold in 1764 to the Prince de Condé who later purchased the nearby mansion known as the Hôtel de Lassay. During the French Revolution, the palace became State property and was used by the Council of the Five Hundred. A semi-circular auditorium was built in 1795 by Jacques Gisors and Emmanuel Leconte. It was altered by Jules de Joly in 1828. Between 1804 and 1807, Napoleon I had a portico of twelve Corinthian columns erected by Bernard Poyet on the façade in the same style as that used on the Madeleine. Thereafter the two buildings faced each other across the Seine in perfect harmony.

Musée d'Orsay

Ⓜ **Solférino or RER Musée d'Orsay**

The Orsay railway station was built underground by Victor Laloux between 1898 and 1900 on the site of the Orsay Palace, built in 1838 and demolished by fire in 1871 during the days of the Paris Commune. The building was inaugurated on 14th July 1900 for the World Fair. Above the station was a 600-bedroom hotel. The façade, flanked by two gigantic clocks, is decorated with allegorical statues representing the towns to which the trains from the Chemins de fer d'Orléans company ran. The station was used from 1900 to 1939 but then gradually fell into disuse because it was too small. The building was due for demolition when it was added to the additional Historic Monuments list in 1978. It was then decided to turn it into a museum of 19th century art, covering works from the 1848-1914 period. Architects Renaud Bardon, Pierre Colboc and Jean-Paul Philippon were responsible for the necessary alterations to the layout. Little remains of the structural design of the old building except for the luxurious hotel reception rooms which Gae Aulenti, an Italian interior designer, very successfully connected with the museum area.

Eight years later, on 1st December 1986, the Musée d'Orsay was officially opened by François Mitterand.

The Church in Auvers-sur-Oise (June 1890) by Vincent van Gogh (1853-1890).

The clock in the main concourse – from station to art gallery.

The façade of the Musée d'Orsay running along Quai Anatole France is 220 metres (715 ft.) long. Carpeaux (1827-1875), Courbet (1819-1877), Gallé (1846-1904), Guimard (1867-1942) and Gauguin (1848-1903) are among the artists well represented in the gallery's collections.

Musée d'Orsay

4

5

1

1 : Poppy Field, *Argenteuil* (1873) by Claude Monet (1840-1926).
2 : *Victor Hugo* (1897) by Auguste Rodin (1840-1917).
3 : *Herakles the Archer* (Bronze, cast in 1924) by Bourdelle (1861-1929).
4 : *Two Young Girls at the Piano* (1892) by Auguste Renoir (1841-1919).
5 : *Self-portrait* (1889) by Vincent van Gogh (1853-1890).
6 : *Thought* (1886-1889) – *A Portrait of Camille Claudel* (1864-1943) - by Auguste Rodin (1840-1917).

2

6

3

The main organ in the church in Saint-Germain-des-Prés.

Tour n°9

Discus Thrower in the Luxembourg Garden.

Institut de France

Pont-Neuf

Institut de France, not far away, was built thanks to a large legacy left by Mazarin. Originally, the money was to be used to build a college for some sixty pupils from the new French provinces, annexed by the Treaty of Westphalia in 1648 and the Peace of the Pyrenees in 1659 (Alsace, Artois, Roussillon and Pignerol in Italy). This explains its name, the "Collège des quatre-Nations". In addition to a college, it was to house the Academy and a library. The construction of the college under Louis le Vau between 1663 and 1670 resulted in a curving frontage flanked by two pavilions decorated with firepots above the attics. The sumptuous cupola bearing the Cardinal's coat-of-arms tops the chapel containing, in the foyer, the donor's black and white marble tomb by Antoine Coysevox. On the death of Le Vau in 1670, it was François d'Orbay who continued the work until the building was completed in 1688.

The college designed by Louis le Vau has a curved façade flanked by two pavilions decorated with firepots above their attics. The sumptuous dome bearing the cardinal's coat-of-arms tops a chapel in whose entrance is the black and white marble tomb of the donor. The tomb was designed by Antoine Coysevox. The Institut also contains the Mazarine Library, the first public library in France, containing Cardinal Mazarin's own collection of books.

Institut de France regroups the five national academies : Académie française founded in 1635 by Richelieu, Académie des inscriptions et belles lettres (1663), the Academy of Science (1666) and the Academy of Fine Arts which has replaced both the Academy of Painting and Sculpture (1648) and the Academy of architecture (1671) in 1818. Those were refounded by Colbert. The Academy of politics and moral sciences was created later in 1795.

The carriage entrance is emblazoned with Louis XV's monogram and its tympanum is decorated with fleur-de-lys. Through this entrance, one gains acess to a hall leading to stairways ornated with splendid laced bannisters.

Hôtel des Monnaies

Pont-Neuf

In 1768, Louis XV decided that a Mint should be built on the banks of the Seine. It was Jacques Denis Antoine (1733-1801), then a total unknown, who won the competition for the tender. Construction began in 1771 and the return of architectural symmetry in 1750 during Louis XV's reign led, during this period, to the use of neo-Classical designs. The new forms created by Gabriel and Soufflot were influenced by the cubic forms and terraced roofs of the English Renaissance which drew its inspiration from the designs of Palladio.

The Mint, completed in 1775, stretches along a length of 114 metres (371 ft.) and covers an area of more than 12,000 sq. metres. Above the attic are allegories of Law, Prudence, Strength, Trade, Abundance and Peace.

The Mint now houses a workshop for coinage in precious metals, a workshop for medals and the Paris Mint Museum.

The Square du Vert Galant gets its name from the nickname (literally, the "Gay Old Spark") given to Henri IV by pamphleteers of the day. The Granst Master of the Order of the Knights of the Temple was burnt at the stake here in 1314 on the orders of Philip the Fair.

Saint-Germain-des-Prés

Saint-Germain -des-Prés

In the 6th century, Childebert I, Clovis' son, and St. Germain, Bishop of Paris, decided to build a church to house St. Vincent's tunic and a gold cross from Toledo. A basilica was erected, followed by a monastery. After the bishop's death in 576 A.D, a pilgrimage was organised to his tomb in St. Symphorien's Chapel near the westwork. The abbey became the final resting-place of Merovingian kings until Dagobert, and as such it enjoyed massive expansion. After the final invasions in the 8th and 9th centuries, the abbey was rebuilt and this coincided with its revival. The westwork on the church in Saint-Germain-des-Prés was built between 990 and 1014. However, the top level was given twin bays strengthened by four corner piers in the 19th century. The nave was built during the 11th century but the vaulting dates from the 17th. The construction of the chancel began c. 1145; it was consecrated in 1163 by Pope Alexander III. The cloister, refectory and dorter were built in the 13th century to designs by Pierre de Montreuil, the architect of the Sainte-Chapelle.

The Saint-Germain-des-Prés district was also one of the favourite haunts of intellectuals such as Apollinaire, Gide, Breton, Giraudoux, Prévert, Sartre, Tzara, Queneau and de Beauvoir who met at the Café de Flore, the Café des Deux Magots and the Brasserie Lipp. After the Liberation of France, Juliette Gréco, Boris Vian and Mouloudji were among those who provided evening entertainment in the district.

1

2

3

4

5

1 : Capital in the transept crossing – 12th century.
2 : Madonna and Child, from Notre-Dame de Paris – 14th century.
3 : A stained-glass window from the refectory – 13th century. Remounted in the 19th century in the second chapel on the south side.
4 : The apse, 12th century.
5 : The 11th-century bell towner.

Right :
To ensure that the music could be heard throughout the church, the nave, side aisles and transept were given ogival vaulting in the early 18th century.

Saint-Sulpice

Saint-Sulpice

The foundation stone was laid by Anne of Austria in 1646. The work, carried out successively by Christophe Guimard, Daniel Gittard then Gilles Marie Oppenord, lasted for almost one hundred years.

In 1732, Jean-Nicholas Servandoni (1695-1766) was commissioned to build the West Front of the church. Instead of superposing the three Orders in a manner that had been fashionable since the beginning of the 17th century, he designed a West Front resembling a Greek temple, introducing a new form of architecture characterised by the antique porticoes.

The nave was completed in 1736 and the towers built by Maclaurin between 1766 and 1770 . Inside, Delacroix' works painted between 1858 and 1863 represent St. Michael slaying the dragon, Heliodorus being chased from the Temple and Jacob fighting the Angel.

The Fontaine des Quatre-Orateurs on Place Saint-Sulpice represents Bossuet, Fénelon, Fléchier and Massillon. It was designed by Louis Visconti and built between 1843 and 1848.

Between 1777 and 1780, the left tower is built by J.F. Chalgrin. The pediment designed by MacLaurin was replaced by the present ballustrade.

A close-up of the Fontaine des Quatre-Orateurs.

Eugène Delacroix, Jacob Fighting the Angel (1858-63).

Saint-Séverin

Saint-Michel

Saint-Séverin was built between the 13th and 14th centuries on the site of a sanctuary known to have existed since the 6th century. Circa 1450, the church was ravaged by fire. All that remained were the tower and first three spans of the nave. Rebuilding began on the church at the end of the 15th century. The chevet and ossuary were completed in 1489; the side chapels between 1498 and 1520. Later, in 1673, Jules Hardouin-Mansart built the oval Communion Chapel to the south-east of the apse.

The door in the West Front dates from the 13th century and comes from the church of Saint-Pierre-aux-Bœufs which was demolished when Rue d'Arcole was laid out on the Ile de la Cité.

Inside, the first three spans in the 13th-century nave are easy to identify because of the huge cylindrical pillars that are so characteristic of the Early Gothic style in the Paris Basin. The 15th-century pillars are lighter and decorated with slender colonnettes; they have no capitals. The chancel is roofed with superb vaulting that includes eighteen cells and seven keystones. It rivals the double Flamboyant Gothic ambulatory with its extraordinary pillars. There is another example of this type of work in Provence, in the scriptorium in Silvacane Abbey. Rising from this pillar like lianas rolled around the column, are the fourteen ribs of the vaulting above the apse. This palm grove in stone is reminiscent of the famous "palm tree" in the Dominicans' church in Toulouse.

La Grande Mademoiselle and the parish priest of Saint-Séverin

The marble décor in the chancel dates from the 17th century and was created by Jean-Baptiste Tuby to designs by Charles Le Brun. It is the Grande Mademoiselle, Duchess of Montpensier, who is thank for it. Her residence, the Luxembourg Palace, stood within the parish of Saint-Sulpice but she had fallen out with the priest there and preferred to pay for marble decoration in her adopted parish.

Cluny-La Sorbonne

The Roman baths of Cluny

The Roman baths date from the 2nd century A.D. The ship's bows on the vaulting suggest that they were reserved for the corporation of boatmen of Lutetia or were gifted to the town by the corporation which was very influential at that time. The frigidarium, or "cold room", has survived intact. It is a large rectangular chamber 20 metres (62 ft.) long and 11 metres (36 ft.) wide with a height of 14 metres (47 ft.). The walls are 2 metres (6 1/2 ft.) thick and built of ashlar rubble with red brick stringing.

Hôtel de Cluny
and Roman baths of Cluny

The Hôtel de Cluny (1485-1498) made use of the Flamboyant Gothic architecture tested from the end of the 14th century onwards in churches and chapels and, thanks to the inclusion of major new features, is a precursor of the Renaissance. The mansion, built for the Abbots of Cluny, consists of two large sections, a chapel and six staircases including one outside the main line of the building decorated with emblems of St. James. The building backs onto the remains of the Roman baths. The mansion was designed by Jacques d'Amboise. The mansion consists of a central building divided by a spiral staircase projecting beyond the main line of the construction. Two buildings, to east and west, close off the inner courtyard. The windows on the first and second floors are mullioned i.e. they have stone crossbars. On the third floor, a balustrade with Flamboyant Gothic tracery decorated with imaginary gargoyles conceals a parapet walkway, included because civil unrest was still very much in everybody's minds. The dormer windows in the attic have gables carved with coats-of-arms and decorated with a veritable piece of lacework in stone strengthened by robust piers carved with picturesque representations of animals.

« The Lady and the Unicorn »

The museum has a very rich collection of medieval art, among which « The Lady and the Unicorn » (15th century), which is in fact made up of six tapestries coming from Boussac castle (Creuse, in Limousin). The first five tapestries symbolise the five senses and the sixth one possibly represents withdrawing from the world.

2

1

Flamboyant Gothic style
In the 15th century, the exteriors of the town houses of the new wealthy middle classes were covered in decorative features on the doorways (3) and window surrounds, dormer windows (1), traceried gables and external spiral staircases (2).

Museum middle ages : Alexandre de Sommerard installed his collection of mediaeval art in the Hôtel de Cluny in 1832, at the time of the closure of the Musée des Petit-Augustins, the first Museum of French Monuments opened during the Revolution by Alexandre Lenoir. Alexandre de Sommerard and Albert Lenoir, the son of Alexandre Lenoir, succeeded in imposing the idea of a museum of "national antiquities". Since then, the museum has boasted an extensive mediaeval art collection including the famous "Lady with the Unicorn" tapestry dating from the 15th century. It actually consists of six tapestries from the Château de Boussac in the département of Creuse. The first five tapestries symbolise the five senses; the sixth is said to symbolise renunciation of the world.

3

Palais du Luxembourg

RER Luxembourg

The Luxembourg Palace was built from 1615 onwards to designs by Salomon de Brosse for Marie de Medici. The design was supposed to remind Louis XIII's mother of the Pitti Palace in Florence, the town of her birth. However, the architect retained the typical layout of 16th-century private mansions i.e. a beautiful house set between courtyard and garden and flanked by two wings.

The interior is luxuriously decorated and the famous series of 24 paintings of The Life of Marie de Medici painted by Rubens for the gallery in the west wing is now kept in the Louvre.
The Luxembourg Palace is now the seat of the Senate.

The Luxembourg Gardens were extensively altered by Jean-François Chalgrin (1739-1811) in the early 19th century. The garden is partly French in style, with beds set out around the large octagonal pond; the remainder, with shrubs and bushes creating winding shadows across adjacent paths, is reminiscent of English landscaping.

Visitors tired by all the walking will find that this is not only a quiet and peaceful place to rest their weary legs but also a place from which to enjoy a breathtaking view of the towers on the Church of St. Sulpitius (Saint-Sulpice), the dome on the Pantheon and cupola of Val-de-Grâce Church with its Baroque ornamentation.

The Medici fountain with its rustic decor is typical of the Louis XIII period. The fountain was relocated in 1866 and completed by Auguste-Louis-Marie Orrin with a statue of Polyphemus preparing to crush Acis the Sicilian shepherd preferred by the goddess Galatea. ▶

The façade, a replica of the original, was built by Alphonse de Gisors between 1835 and 1841 to balance the other side of the building. ▼

Panthéon
and the Latin Quarter

Cardinal-Lemoine or RER Luxembourg

In Louis XV's reign, religious architecture did not create any real style; it continued to make use of the Jesuit model developed during the reign of Louis XIII and seen, for example, in the West Front of St. Roch's Church (1739) which was designed by Robert de Cotte (1656-1735). However, the design of West Fronts in the style of Greek temples and the non-use of superimposed orders paved the way for a new architectural concept resulting in the introduction of the ancient portico. St. Genevieve's Church, begun in 1764 to designs by Jacques-Germain Soufflot (1713-1780), was laid out with this ornamental ideal in mind.

The West Front, which was completed in 1775, consists mainly of columns. The church is laid out in the shape of a Greek cross 110 metres long and 82 metres wide. The floor-to-ceiling height is more than 80 metres. Inside are frescoes by Puvis de Chavannes representing the Life of St. Genevieve and by Antoine Jean-Gros who decorated the dome with paintings of the Apotheosis of St. Genevieve. Soufflot died before the end of the building work and was replaced by Brébion and Rondelet (1743-1829), who completed the building in 1790. The pediment above the peristyle was by David; it dates from 1831. The French Revolution turned the church into a pantheon dedicated to the country's great men. Mirabeau, Voltaire, Rousseau, Hugo, Jean Moulin and Malraux are all buried here.

The pediment above the peristyle on the Pantheon was carved by David in 1831. ►

◄ The interior houses frescoes by Puvis de Chavannes representing the Life of St. Genevieve. Work by Antoine Jean-Gros decorates the cupola. The paintings illustrate the Apotheosis of St. Genevieve.

In thanks for his recovery during the siege of Metz in 1744, Louis XV promised to build a church on the location of an ancien shrine dedicated to St. Genevieve, patron saint of Paris.

Chapel in the Sorbonne by Jacques Le Mercier (1635-1642). ►

St. Michael's Fountain (Fontaine Saint-Michel) by Gabriel Davioud (1858-1860). ▼

The Latin Quarter lies between Saint-Germain-des-Prés and the Luxeumbourg Palace. However, the heart of this district lies at the Sorbonne. The Latin Quarter includes the Sorbonne, the Collège de France, St. Genevieve library, well-known junior and senior high schools and a number of the country's leading higher education establishments such as Ecole des Mines (engineering college), les Beaux-Arts (art school), École normale supérieure (college providing training for high-level administrative positions) etc. The district gets its name from the lectures given in Latin in mediaeval universities.

AUX GRANDS HOMMES LA PATRIE RECONNAISSANTE

Saint-Étienne-du-Mont

Cardinal-Lemoine or RER Luxembourg

The old abbey cloister is decorated with 17th-century stained glass.

The church of "St. Stephen on the Hill" was built from 1222 onwards near the minster in St. Genevieve's Abbey, and rebuilt from 1492 to 1586. The main entrance was not completed until 1622.

The roodscreen in Saint-Etienne-du-Mont is the only such screen to have survived intact in Paris. It was built between 1530 and 1545. The decoration on the screen dates from the Renaissance and resolutely turns its back on Gothic art and architecture. The Corinthian Order, foliage, scrolls, grotesques, fruit and figures of Fame were used from the early 16th century onwards.

1

2

3

4

1 : Appearing to the disciples on the road to Emmaus.
2 : Noah's Ark.
3 : Manna in the desert.
4 : Jewish Feast of Passover.

During "St. Genevieve's nine day week" beginning on 3rd January, the saint's relics are placed on show and venerated by crowds of pilgrims. Margaret of Valois, nicknamed Queen Margot, made a donation of 3000 pounds for the building of the façade. She laid the first stone in 1610.

A Renaissance roodscreen (1530-1545). ▼

Saint-Julien-le-Pauvre

Maubert-Mutualité or Saint-Michel-Notre-Dame

The Church of St. Julian the Pauper was built between 1165 and circa 1220 by Benedictine monks from Longpont. Shortly after the reign of St. Louis, the schools around Notre-Dame relocated to the left bank and joined together to form a university. The seat of the new institution, Alma Parens, which dispensed Christian thought and knowledge, was set up in the church until 1525.

The building began to fall into a decline in the middle of the 16th century. By the middle of the 17th century, the first two spans had become dangerous and had to be demolished. The church lost its status as a priory in 1658 and became a daughter chapel to Saint-Séverin. It was shut down during the French Revolution then restored thanks to renewed interest in historic monuments in the 19th century. It was allocated to the hospital (Hôtel-Dieu) when it reopened in 1826. In 1889, it became a place of Greek Melchite worship (Greek Catholicism). An iconostasis wall now separates the nave from the sanctuary as required by this form of worship.

Since the 6th century, several churches and chapels have stood on this site, which lay at the intersection of two very busy Roman roads - Rue Saint-Jacques, the road to Orléans, and Rue Galante, the road to Lyon and Italy. The Petit-pont (bridge) was also nearby, providing a link across the Seine to the Ile de la Cité. A night hospice for travellers was not far away.

The Lutetia arena

Rue Mouffetard and Saint-Médard

Place Monge

Rue Mouffetard is one of the most picturesque streets in Paris. It runs from Saint-Médard to Place de la Contrescarpe.

St. Médard's Church was built on the site of a Merovingian church dedicated to a saint who was Bishop of Soissons and close to Kings Clothar I and Chilperic I. Like St. Genevieve's Abbey of which it was a daughter church, St. Medard's stood on the Roman road to Lyon. The present church was built during three different historical periods. The nave and side aisles were built in the late 15th century; the chancel was added in the 16th.

▲ The ***Lutetia Arena,*** located at 6 Rue des Arènes (Monge subway station), was built towards the end of the 1st century B.C. It would be more correct to describe it as an amphitheatre since this is the term used by experts to describe an arena surrounded by tiers of seats. 15,000 spectators could take their places here but the arena was destroyed during the Barbarian invasions of the 3rd century. The site was gradually covered over and abandoned, and was not rediscoverd until much later, when Rue Monge was being laid out in 1869.

Muséum National d'Histoire Naturelle and Jardin des Plantes

In 1633, Louis XIII purchased the 24 acres that made up the Cloypeau estate in order to have a royal garden of medicinal plants laid out there. Guy de La Brosse, physician ordinary to the king, was responsible for it from 1633 to 1640. The king's doctors then succeeded each other as head of the royal garden until the arrival of the Count de Buffon who has remained the best-known of all the garden's supervisors to the present day. He managed the garden from 1739 to 1788, doubling its size by adding the land between the original garden and the Seine. During the French Revolution, the royal garden underwent a complete redesign and became the Museum of Natural History (Muséum d'histoire naturelle). A menagerie was created to house the last animals from the royal menagerie at Versailles.

Three major galleries :

The Grand Gallery depicting changes in the living world (1877-1889) was built by Jules André. It was closed in 1965 for security reasons was not reopened until 1994 after it had been redesigned by Paul Chemetov and Borja Huidobro, who were also the architects of the Ministry of Finance in Bercy.

The Paleontology Gallery contains a vast ossuary housing the skeletons of some 36,000 vertebrates. The building erected by Fernand Dutert between 1894 and 1895 is decorated with bronze and marble low reliefs and statues of naturalists.

The Mineralogy Gallery contains a collection of minerals ranging from the most common-place to the most precious. In all, more than 500,000 exhibits are on display. It was Rohault de Fleury who designed the building in 1836.

Gare-d'Austerlitz

The national natural history museum includes a garden that is a maze of plants and shrubs, a school, glasshouses, an alpine garden, a menagerie, several laboratories and a number of galleries.

The Grand Gallery.

La Pitié-Salpêtrière

Austerlitz

In 1656 Louis XIV decided to build a vast "general hospice" in accordance with an edict signed by Louis XIII, to provide accommodation for sick beggars and the infirm who, in return, would work there. The institution was opened and consisted of several different establishments. La Salpêtrière, which is one of them, was built over an old powder magazine that provided supplies to the Arsenal on the other side of the Seine.

At the end of the 17th century a "remand centre" for prostitutes and young girls of dubious virtue was added to the hospice. It continued to operate until the 19th century then lost its function as a place of internment and thereafter merely provided health care.

The women in La Salpêtrière were released in 1792 by a gang of crooks. The release turned into a riot and dozens of women were raped and killed. The "remand centre" was closed for ever after this massacre. After 1796, the hospital was used as a mental asylum.

Louis le Vau designed ambitious plans between 1657 and 1670, when he was seconded by architects Paul-Marie Duval and Pierre Le Muet. When Le Vau died, Libéral Bruant was commissioned to design the chapel (1670-1677). His layout took the form of a Greek Cross. The transept crossing was roofed with a polygonal cupola supported by a drum pierced with windows. The High Alter was placed in the central rotunda and could be seen by approximately 4,000 people who were easy to monitor, in separate compartments. He also designed the façades and the dome.

The pavilions in La Salpêtrière have been altered regularly since the 17th century. They are linked by a network of underground passages.

Libéral Bruant (1636-1697) was one of the most important architects of the French Classical period. He was given the title of architect royal in 1663 and became a member of the Académie royale d'architecture when it was set up in 1671. He designed the Hôtel des Invalides in Paris.

The Montparnasse district with, at its centre, a tower block 210 metres high.

Tour n°10

Saint-Denis in Notre-Dame-des-Champs on Boulevard Montparnasse.

Montparnasse and Port Royal

RER Port-Royal

The **Observatory Fountain**, also known as the fountain of the "four corners of the globe" was designed by Gabriel Davioud, Jean-Baptiste Carpeaux and Emmanuel Frémiet. It was unveiled in 1875.

Port-Royal
The Cistercian abbey of Port-Royal-des-Champs created a new house in Paris in 1626. Twenty years later, Antoine Le Pautre designed the superb chapel. Today, the buildings house the Port-Royal Maternity Clinic.

The name "Montparnasse" was given to the district by students from the Latin Quarter who, in the 17th century, came to recite poetry on a manmade mound that was razed in the 18th century. The mound referred back to Mount Parnassus, dedicated to Apollo and the Muses of Greek mythology.

Like Montmartre, Montparnasse attracted artists, including Picasso, Foujita, Soutine, Modigliani, Léger, Gris, Chagall, Matisse and Giacometti, to name but a few. The district was just being built and rents were competitive. The cafés were cheap and they created a lively bustle centred on the artists' community that was to become known as the "Paris School".

Val-de-Grâce

RER Port-Royal

Anne of Austria, Louis XIII's young wife, purchased the Petit-Bourbon Estate in 1621. On it, she commissioned the building of a convent to which she brought Benedictine nuns from the Abbaye du Val-Profond in Essonne. The queen was a regular visitor to the small pavilion which she had had built for herself and she promised to commission a superb church upon the birth of her heir. In 1638, the future Louis XIV was born. The foundation stone was laid on 1st April 1645 by the young Louis XIV and the work was entrusted to François Mansart, later replaced by Jacques Lemercier who had already built the chapel in the Sorbonne. Pierre Le Muet took over the work on Lemercier's death in 1654 but it was Louis Le Duc who built the dome on Val-de-Grâce, still using Mansart's plans.

The Corinthian nave has three bays flanked by side chapels. The arches, vaulting and ribbed arches are decorated with pious carvings by sculptor Michel Anguier. The chancel has a canopy with twisted columns in the style of St. Peter's in Rome and the cupola over squinches is decorated with paintings by Mignard dating from 1663. It represents, in the middle of a crowd of saints and martyrs, Anne of Austria being led by her son, and St. Anne offering Val-de-Grâce to God. The work comes to a halt in 1669 upon Le Muet's death.

The dome on a stormy afternoon.

Val-de-Grâce

The nave.

The ***entrance to Val-de-Grâce*** consists of two superimposed orders topped by a triangular pediment above two volutes. The dome is decorated with fire pots, statues of children and elegant bell turrets. The Sorbonne Church, built by Jacques Lemercier between 1635 and 1642, is in the same style. This type of façade has its own special character, imitating 16th-century Italian religious architecture reminiscent of the Gesù Church in Rome on which building began in 1568.

General view of Val-de-Grâce Abbey.

Observatoire de Paris

RER Port-Royal

The Observatory was commissioned by Louis XIV from architect Claude Perrault between 1668 and 1672. The north-south line of the building corresponds to the Paris meridian, which was later abandoned in favour of the Greenwich meridian. The Observatory is a vast rectangle 31.22 metres long and 28.62 metres wide. The four sides correspond to the four cardinal points. Two octagonal towers stand adjacent to the building and it was not until the 19th century that a dome was built on top of the eastern tower to house an astronomical telescope.

The Paris meridian is represented by 135 bronze medallions sealed into the pavements of Paris by Dutch artist Jan Dibbets in 1994. These 135 medallions commemorate François Arago, a scientist, politician and former Director of Observations. His bronze statue, which once stood on Place de l'Île de Sein, was melted down in 1942.

Two trophies decorated with globes and astronomical instruments adorn the south side, which is flan

Denfert-Rochereau

© Dac – Christophe Fouin

The catacombs.

Bartholdi's sculpture in the centre of Place Denfert-Rochereau is a smaller bronze replica of the Belfort Lion carved into a wall of rock in Belfort in honour of Colonel Denfert-Rochereau who defended the town during the Franco-Prussian War of 1870. The sculpture was unveiled in 1880.

Place Denfert-Rochereau

The catacombs

Denfert-Rochereau

Note the houses round Place Denfert-Rochereau (1784-1787). The entrance to the Catacombs is in the pavilion at No. 2. These pavilions serve as a reminder of the Farmer Generals' Wall built around Paris (cf. page 64).

© Dac – Christophe Fouin

The catacombs are old stone quarries used to store bones from Parisian graveyards that have been closed.

The Palace of Versailles overlooking the park.

Tour n°11

Louis XIV by Hyacinthe Rigaud - 1701.

Château de Vincennes

Château-de-Vincennes

Charles V, King of France between 1364 and 1380, had a Chapel Royal built. In 1369, work was completed on a keep 52 metres (169 ft.) high on which construction had started during his father's reign, in 1361. He also commissioned the building of an enormous outer wall measuring 378 metres by 175 metres (410 yds. by 190 yds.) between 1373 and 1377.

At the beginning of the 17th century, Vincennes was nothing more than an old mediaeval castle by comparison with modern residences such as the Tuileries Palace, the Louvre or the castle in Blois. The fortress remained in use as a prison and, occasionally, provided a refuge for the Court. During the Regency, Mazarin turned Vincennes into a modern royal residence, redeveloping the old mediaeval castle by adding, in 1654 and 1658, two wings in the Classical style. The aim was to provide protection against attack from outside without giving an impression of undue confinement.

1

1 : The keep ; 2 : The wall; 3 : The keep and the arcaded wall ; 4 : The outer wall ; 5 and 6 : Work began on the Sainte-Chapelle during the reign of Charles V. Charles VI (1380-1422) commissioned Jean Amiot to continue to project and it would appear to be this architect who completed the huge bays in 1400. However, it was not until François I's reign (1515-1547) that work started again in earnest and the building was completed during the reign of his successor, Henri II, in 1552.

The princes and leading noblemen were accommodated in the grand North and South Wings. Courtiers lived in the apartments on the town side of the palace. The king and queen occupied the first floor of the central building.

2

5

3

4

6

Basilica Saint-Denis

Basilique-Saint-Denis

The basilica church is 108 metres (351 ft.) long, the transept is 39 metres (127 ft.) wide and the height up to the vaulted roof is 29 metres (94 ft.). The south tower rises to a height of 58 metres (189 ft.). The north steeple, which was 84 metres (273 ft.) tall, was destroyed. Louis IX officially established a royal burial place in 1264 when it was decided to place the bodies of sovereigns in richly decorated tombs in the transept of the minster. King Dagobert was the first king to be buried in Saint-Denis.

1 : Tomb of Charles V the Wise.
2 : Mausoleum of Louis XVI and Marie-Antoinette.
3 : West Front of the nave.
4 : West Front.

The building, which had already undergone alterations in the Carolingian period, was again rebuilt during the reign of Louis VII at the instigation of Suger, abbot of the monastery and minister to the monarch. In 1135, the Abbot ordered the rebuilding of the West Front on the minster. The three entrances, with their column-statues, were completed in 1140 and mark the beginnings of Gothic architecture in France. The tympanum on the central doorway represents the Last Judgement, the tympanum on the left the martyrdom of St. Dennis and the one on the right his last Communion. Nothing is left of the twenty statue-columns; they were destroyed during the French Revolution.

The second innovation was the double ambulatory built between 1140 and 1144. The use of intersecting ribbed vaulting made it possible to include wide bays in the chevet. The chancel, flooded with light, was also to be as spacious as possible to enable large numbers of believers to approach the Holy Relics and the basilica's most sacred artefacts without crowding and jostling.

When Suger died, the minster was still not finished and the Carolingian nave was in a poor state of repair. It was not until 1231 that Pierre de Montreuil began to build the three storeys in the nave with arching, triforium, clerestory and transept. This work was completed in 1241.

1

2

3

4

Versailles

RER C or SNCF from Gare Montparnasse

Since 1624, Louis XIII had had a hunting lodge in the middle of the well-stocked Forest of Versailles. In 1631, he asked his architect, Philibert Le Roy, to build him a larger palace on this spot, using white stone and red bricks, and to include a tall roof of black slate. The modest castle consisted of central apartments and two wings set at right angles to them.

After overcoming the dangers of the Fronde Revolt, Louis XIV looked for ways of restoring royal authority to its full glory. In 1661, he commissioned Le Vau the architect, Le Brun the interior designer, and Le Nôtre the landscape gardener to give his father's outmoded castle a new, brilliant lease of life.

In 1668, Le Vau surrounded the three sides of Louis XIII's U-shaped castle with a sumptuous Classical façade.

Jules Hardouin-Mansart succeeded Le Vau in 1678 and launched a long-term building project for the construction of two wings on the garden side, the "South Wing" and the "North Wing", flanking the central section. Four years later, Louis XIV officially moved to Versailles. In 1699, the architect began building work on the chapel royal; it was comp leted by his brother-in-law, Robert de Cotte, in 1710.

On the death of Louis XIV, the court left Versailles and did not return until seven years later when Louis XV decided to use it as his main residence. Jacques-Ange Gabriel made extensive alterations to the royal apartments and, in 1770, completed the royal opera house, built entirely of carved wood and fake painted marble.

The side of the castle overlooking the garden. Masks, allegorical and mythological divinities from the days of the Ancient Greeks and Romans, warlike trophies and firepots dominate the external decoration. A balustraded attic can be seen right at the top of the building.

The Marble Courtyard.

The façade overlooking the park, which was completed by Jules Hardouin-Mansart in 1689, consists of two long symmetrical wings facing onto the gardens. They have a basements with rounded windows and a first floor with columns, decorated with trophies consising of weapons and carved allegories. Masks, allegorical and mythological allegories of Ancient Greece and Rome, warlike trophies, and firepots dominate the external decoration. On roof level is an attic with balustrades. ▼

The garden, the Grand Trianon and the Petit Trianon

In 1666, Louis XIV ordered Le Nôtre to lay out grandiose vistas highlighting the fountains and statues dotted here and there in avenues and thickets. It took extensive earthworks and drainage to turn the thankless site into Louis XIV's favourite place for a stroll. The first decorative features to be installed, e.g. the Basins of the Seasons, were made of lead. Later, marble was chosen, for example in 1674 for the Grand Order of 24 statues placed at Colbert's initiative to designs by Lebrun and students at the Académie de France in Rome. The bronze decorations appeared from 1685 onwards. The statues of rivers and combats in the Animals' Cabinet date from this period.

After 1687, Hardouin-Mansart built the Grand Trianon as a place in which the king and Madame de Maintenon could rest and relax. The columns and pilasters were made of pink Languedoc marble.

It was Louis XV who had the Petit Trianon built in 1762, to designs by Gabriel, for Madame de Pompadour. The king's mistress, however, died before it was inaugurated in 1764.

Marie-Antoinette ordered extensive alterations to the Trianon Park in 1777 and commissioned Richard Mique to build her a hamlet consisting of thatched or tiled cottages. The "farm", which resembles a stage set, included a dairy, a fishery and a mill.

Queen Marie-Antoinette's hamlet.

1

4

5

2

3

6

1: The Petit Trianon introduced the fashion of small pavilions sweetly known as "follies". It was Louis XV who commissioned this small building from Gabriel for Madame de Pompadour in 1762. 2: A faun playing the flute - Simon Hurtrelle. 3: The Temple of Love (1778). 4: The Grand Trianon. 5: Group sculpture of Laocoon and his sons (1696). 6: The fountains in the Apollo Basin.

SNCF from Gare de Lyon

The castle seen from the flower gardens.

East Wing overlooking the White Horse Courtyard. Philibert Delorme designed the first horseshoe-shaped steps in the so-called "White Horse courtyard". Jean Androuet du Cerceau rebuilt it in 1632.

Fontainebleau

The foundation of the castle is said to date back to the reign of Louis VI (1108-1137) or even the reign of Philip I (1060-1108). In 1259, St. Louis grantedFontainebleau to monks from the Order of the Holy Trinity who built a chapel and a hospice for the poor. In the 14th and 15th centuries, the castle received regular visits from French monarchs but they lost interest in it after 1450, preferring the luxurious residences on the banks of the River Loire.

The residence was totally redesigned when King François I returned from captivity in 1526. In 1528, the work was entrusted to Master Mason Gilles Le Breton. The mediaeval foundations and the great 12th-century tower were retained in memory of St. Louis, who had lived here. On the other hand, nothing was left of the abbey buildings used by the Trinitarians.

1

3

2

1 : View of the castle with the Lake Pavilion dating from Louis XIV's reign in the foreground.

2 and 3 : François I Gallery.

A prestigious gallery, the François I Gallery, was built between 1535 and 1539. The interior decoration was commissioned from the Florentine artist Jean-Baptiste Rosso and the Bolognese artist Francesco Primaticcio. Together, they created the first Fontainebleau School.

The west end of the castle was completed during the reign of Henri II (1547-1559) and the east end during that of Henri IV (1589-1610) when Fontainebleau again became a major centre for the Arts and the second Fontainebleau School was founded, led by Toussaint Dubreuil and Martin Fréminet.

The castle was a popular residence before the French Revolution and underwent regular alterations by monarchs and emperors from Louis XIII to Napoleon III.

Saint-Germain en Laye

RER A1

Louis VI the Fat had the first castle built in Saint-Germain en Laye circa 1124. Philip Augustus regularly resided at the castle and St. Louis added a chapel to it before 1238. The St. Louis Chapel was designed by architect Pierre de Montreuil but has undergone many alterations since that time. Painted decoration and works by Nicolas Poussin and Simon Vouet were added.

King Edward III of England set fire to the castle in 1346 but spared the chapel. Charles V had it rebuilt between 1364 and 1367. The Valois family then abandoned the place until 1539, when François I began his rebuilding over the foundations of the old castle. The work was commissioned from Pierre Chambiges, succeeded on his death in 1544 by Guillaume Guillain and Jean Langeois. The structural work was completed in 1547, the year in which François I died. Henri II and architect Philibert Delorme continued the project.

The chapel is 27 metres long and 9.50 metres wide with a floor-to-ceiling height of 17 metres.

Louis XIV was born in 1638 at the Château Neuf. He then lived in the Château Vieux with the Queen, the Duchess de La Vallière and the Marquise de Montespan until he moved away to the splendours of Versailles.

The origin of the "New Castle" was a "Theatre House" designed by Philibert Delorme for Henri II in 1550. The extension to this building was to become the New Castle on which construction work began in 1557 and stopped two years later. Work began again in 1567 then in 1590, and the New Castle was completed by Métezeau and Androuet du Cerceau during Henri IV's reign. Today, all that remains of the New Castle is the Henri IV Pavilion.

The Old Castle was gradually abandoned until the reign of Louis XIV who ordered two lots of work from 1660 onwards. The first contract involved the layout of the gardens by Le Nôtre. Entire beds of box and flowering plants were placed between the New and Old Castles until 1673. The second set of work was commissioned from Jules Hardouin-Mansart between 1682 and 1684. The five cube-shaped pavilions that he added to each of the corners of the Old Castle were demolished in the mid 19th century. In 1862 the castle underwent restoration and, since then, it has housed the National Antiquities Museum (musée des Antiquités nationales) which illustrates the presence of Man in this territory from prehistoric times to the reign of the Merovingian kings.

Château de Malmaison

RER A1

The Château de Malmaison was built circa 1610-1620 for Christophe Perrot, counsellor to the Parliament of Paris. It was twice extended, once in 1686-87 then again in 1780. Malmaison was purchased by Josephine, wife of General Bonaparte, in 1799 and from 1800 to 1802 she had alterations made to the property by architects Charles Percier and Pierre Fontaine. They added the entrance tent, the columns and pilasters, and the Greco-Roman murals in the old apartments.

The English-style park designed by Louis-Martin Berthault and the hothouse ordered by Josephine in 1804 from Jean-Marie Morel were completed in 1805. Maintenance of the greenhouse, however, was too expensive and it was demolished in 1827.

Having been abandoned during the early years of the Empire, Josephine retired to the château after her divorce from Emperor Napoleon in 1809 and continued to live there until she died in 1814.

Château de Vaux-le-Vicomte

SNCF from gare de Lyon or RER D. Gare de Melun

Louis Le Vau created his masterpiece in Vaux-le-Vicomte between 1656 and 1661. This was a foretaste of the Palace of Versailles, providing a generous interpretation of a style of architecture designed for merrymaking and a garden setting.

It was in 1641 that Master of Requests Nicolas Fouquet purchased the Vaux estate and its small fortified castle. Appointed Chief Public Prosecutor to the Parliament of Paris then, later, Superintendent of Finances, a position which he held on his own from 1655, Nicolas Fouquet saw a considerable increase in his income and fortune. He therefore decided to build a new castle, commissioning the services of architect Louis Le Vau, artist Charles Le Brun and gardener André Le Nôtre.

On 17th August 1661, Fouquet hosted festivities in honour of Louis XIV. On 5th September, the king had him arrested. Although the sovereign was jealous of the upturn in his Superintendant's finances and suspected him of embezzlement, it was undoubtedly the public jostling between Colbert and Fouquet for the job previously occupied by Cardinal Mazarin which led to Fouquet's downfall. He was accused of excessive outbursts and ostentatiousness and was imprisoned in Pignerol in Piedmont until his death.

Although Vaux-le-Vicomte is a forerunner of the dramatic design of Versailles, it nevertheless retains traces of the influence and style of Louis XIII's architects, Salomon de Brosse and François Mansart. The layout is compact, with two pavilions on each side, Mansart roofs and a carved pediment above the projecting part of the main building, still decorated with the drum bossages that were so characteristic of the style of Louis XIII's day.
On the other hand, architect Louis le Vau's inventiveness can be seen in the rotunda housing the great oval reception room overlooking the garden. The idea for the rotunda may have been based on the Barberini Palace in Rome.

Contents

Ce livre a été imprimé et broché par POLLINA, 85400 Luçon - n°L63655.
Imprimé en France

IMPRIM'VERT®